SPARKNOTES™

5 Practice Tests for the SAT II Math IC

2003 Edition

Editorial Director Justin Kestler

Executive Editor Ben Florman

Managing Editor Vince Janoski

Technical Director Tammy Hepps

Series Editor John Crowther

Editor Anthony Keene

Contributing Editor Jen Chu

This edition published by Spark Publishing.

Spark Publishing
A Division of SparkNotes LLC
120 Fifth Avenue, 8th Floor
New York, NY 10011

Please submit all comments and questions or report errors to www.sparknotes.com/errors

Library of Congress information available upon request

Printed and bound in Canada

ISBN 1-58663-868-8

SparkNotes is neither affiliated with nor endorsed by Harvard University.

Welcome to SparkNotes Test Preparation

I F YOU WANT TO SCORE HIGH ON THE SAT II MATH IC, YOU NEED TO KNOW more than just the material—you need to know how to take the test. Practice tests are the most effective method for learning the ins and outs of the test. But practice tests that accurately reflect the actual SAT II Math IC have been hard to find—until now. *5 More Practice Tests for the SAT II Math IC* is the first book anywhere dedicated to giving you accurate practice tests so you can perfect your test-taking skills. This book contains:

- **Five full-length SAT II Math IC tests.** The practice tests in this book are the most accurate, true-to-life tests available. Our experts, who've been teaching the SAT II Math IC for years, researched the exam extensively so they could give you tests that reflect exactly what you'll see at the test center. Our tests replicate the format and content of the actual test so closely that nothing will catch you off guard on test day.

- **Clear, helpful explanations for every question—so you can study smarter.** Our explanations do more than tell you the right answer—they identify flaws in your thinking and show you exactly what topics you need to work on. We help you pinpoint your weaknesses, so you can make your studying more efficient by going straight to the stuff you need to review.

- **Specific, proven strategies for the SAT II Math IC.** We give you smart, easy strategies on the best ways to guess, pace yourself, and find shortcuts to answers. These strategies help you maximize your score by showing you how to avoid the test's traps and turn the test's format to your own advantage.

Contents

Orientation

Introduction to the SAT II Tests 3

Colleges and the SAT II Subject Tests 4
Scoring the SAT II Subject Tests 5
Which SAT II Subject Tests to Take 6
When to Take an SAT II Subject Test 10

Introduction to the SAT II Math IC 13

Content of the SAT II Math IC 13
Format of the SAT II Math IC 16
The Calculator 16
Scoring the SAT II Math IC 17

Strategies for the SAT II Math IC 21

Basic Rules of SAT II Test-Taking 21
The Importance of the Order of Difficulty 23
Math Questions and Time 24
Making Your Calculator Work for You 26
Approaching Math IC Questions 30
Guessing and the Math IC 32
Pacing 34

Practice Tests

Practice Tests Are Your Best Friends **39**

Using the Similarity of the SAT II Math IC for Personal Gain 39
Taking a Practice Test 41
Studying Your Practice Test 43
The Secret Weapon: Talking to Yourself 44

SAT II Math IC Practice Test 1 . . . . **47**

SAT II Math IC Practice Test 1 Explanations **63**

SAT II Math IC Practice Test 2 . . . . **.85**

SAT II Math IC Practice Test 2 Explanations **103**

SAT II Math IC Practice Test 3 . . . . **123**

SAT II Math IC Practice Test 3 Explanations **141**

SAT II Math IC Practice Test 4 . . . . **159**

SAT II Math IC Practice Test 4 Explanations **177**

SAT II Math IC Practice Test 5 . . . . **197**

SAT II Math IC Practice Test 5 Explanations **215**

Orientation

Introduction to the SAT II Tests

THE SAT II SUBJECT TESTS ARE CREATED and administered by the College Board and the Educational Testing Service (ETS), the two organizations responsible for producing the dreaded SAT I, which most people just call the SAT. The SAT II Subject Tests were created to act as complements to the SAT I. Whereas the three-hour-long SAT I assesses your critical thinking skills by asking math and verbal questions, the one-hour SAT II Subject Tests examine your knowledge of particular subjects, such as math, writing, and biology.

In our opinion, the SAT II Subject Tests are better tests than the SAT I because they cover clearly-defined topics rather than an ambiguous set of critical-thinking skills. However, just because the SAT II Subject Tests do a better job of testing your actual knowledge than the SAT I does, they are not necessarily easier. A "better" test is not necessarily "better for you" in terms of how easy it will be or how much you need to study.

In comparison to the SAT I, there are good and bad things about the SAT II Subject Tests.

The Good

- Because SAT II Subject Tests cover concrete topics like math, biology, and U.S. history, you can effectively study for them. If you don't know a topic in math, such as how to find the slope of a line, you can easily look it up. In other words, the SAT II tests are straightforward tests: if you know your stuff, you will do well on them.

- Often, the classes you've taken in school have already prepared you well for the test. If you've taken two years of algebra and a year of geometry, you have probably studied most of the topics covered by the SAT II Math IC.

- In preparing for the Math, History, and Chemistry SAT II tests, you really are learning math, history, and chemistry. In other words, you are gaining valuable, even interesting knowledge. If learning is something you enjoy, you might actually find the process of studying for an SAT II test to be worthwhile and gratifying. Few can say the same about studying for the SAT I.

The Bad

Because SAT II Subject Tests quiz you on specific knowledge, it is much harder to "beat" or "outsmart" an SAT II test than it is to outsmart the SAT I. For the SAT I, you can use all sorts of tricks or strategies to figure out an answer. There are far fewer strategies to help you on the SAT II. Don't get us wrong: having test-taking skills will help you on an SAT II, but knowing the subject will help you much more. To do well on the SAT II, you can't just rely on your natural smarts and wits. You need to study.

Colleges and the SAT II Subject Tests

Stop for a second and think about why you would take an SAT II Subject Test. Is it to prove to yourself how much you've learned in the year? That seems unlikely. Is it to prove to your teacher how much you've learned? You've got finals for that. Is it to win you a new car? You wish. No, there's only one reason to take an SAT II Subject Test: colleges want and sometimes require you to.

Colleges care about SAT II Subject Tests for two related reasons. First, the tests demonstrate your interest, knowledge, and skill in specific topics. Second, because SAT II tests are standardized, they show how your skill in math (or biology or writing) measures against the skills of high school students nationwide. The grades you get in high school don't offer such a measurement to colleges: some high schools are more difficult than others, so students of equal ability might receive different grades from different schools. SAT II tests provide colleges with a reliable yardstick against which colleges can measure your—and every other applicant's—knowledge and skills.

When it comes down to it, colleges like the SAT II tests because the tests make the colleges' job easier. The tests are tools the colleges use to compare and evaluate students. But because you know how colleges use the SAT II, you can make the tests *your* tool as well. Since colleges will use your SAT II scores to compare you against other applicants, the tests provide an excellent opportunity to shine. If you get a 93 in Math, and some kid in another high school across the country gets a 91, colleges won't necessarily know what to make of that difference. They don't know whose class is harder or whose teacher is a tough grader or whose high school inflates grades. But if you get a 720 on the SAT II Math IC, and that other kid gets a 650, colleges will recognize the difference in your scores.

The Importance of SAT II Tests in College Applications

Time for some perspective: SAT II tests are *not* the primary tools that colleges use to decide whether to admit an applicant. High school grades, extracurricular activities, and SAT I or ACT scores are all more important to colleges than your scores on SAT II tests. If you take AP tests, those scores will also be more important to colleges than your SAT II scores. But because SAT II tests provide colleges with such a nice and easy measurement tool, they are an important *part* of your application to college. Good SAT II scores can give your application the extra shove that pushes you from the maybe pile into the accepted pile.

College Placement

Occasionally, colleges use SAT II tests to determine placement. For example, if you do very well on the SAT II Math IC, you might be exempted from a basic math class. Though colleges do not often use SAT II tests for placement purposes, it's worth finding out whether the colleges to which you are applying do.

Scoring the SAT II Subject Tests

There are three different names for your SAT II Math IC score. The "raw score" is a simple score of how you did on the test, like the grade you might receive on a normal test in school. The "percentile score" takes your raw score and compares it to the rest of the raw scores in the country for the same test. Percentile scores let you know how you did on the test in comparison to your peers. The "scaled score," which ranges from 200–800, compares your score to the scores received by all students who have ever taken that particular SAT II.

The Raw Score

You will never see your SAT II raw score because the raw score is not included in the SAT II score report. But you should understand how it is calculated, since this knowledge can affect your strategy on the test.

A student's raw score is based entirely on the number of questions that student got right, got wrong, or left blank. You earn one point for every right answer; you lose $\frac{1}{4}$ of a point for every wrong answer; you get no points for questions left blank.

Calculating the raw score is easy. Simply add up the number of questions you answered correctly and the number of questions answered incorrectly. Then multiply the number of wrong answers by ¼, and subtract this value from the number of right answers:

$$\text{raw score} = (\text{correct answers}) - \left(\frac{1}{4} \times \text{wrong answers}\right)$$

In the chapter called "Strategies for the SAT II Math IC," we'll discuss how the rules for calculating a raw score should influence your strategies for guessing and leaving questions blank.

Percentiles

A student's percentile is based on the percentage of the total test-takers who received a lower raw score than he or she did. Say, for example, you had a friend named Pierre Fermat who received a score that placed him in the 83rd percentile. His percentile score tells him that he scored better on the Math IC than 82% of the other students who took the same test. It also means that 17% of the students taking that test scored as well or better than Pierre did.

The Scaled Score

The scaled score takes the raw score and uses a formula to place it onto the standard SAT II scale of 200–800. The curve to convert raw scores to scaled scores differs from test to test. For example, a raw score of 33 on the Math IC might scale to a 600 while the same raw score of 33 on the Math IIC might scale to a 700. In fact, the scaled score can even vary on different editions of the *same* test. A raw score of 33 on the February 2003 Math IC might scale to a 610, while a 33 in June 2003 might scale to a 590. These differences in scaled scores reflect differences in the difficulty level from edition to edition. The difference in the curve for various versions of the same test will not vary by more than 20 points or so.

Which SAT II Subject Tests to Take

There are three types of SAT II tests: those you *must* take, those you *should* take, and those you *shouldn't* take.

- The SAT II tests you must take are those that are required by the colleges you are interested in.

- The SAT II tests you should take are tests that aren't required but that you'll do well on, thereby impressing the colleges looking at your application.

- You shouldn't take the SAT II tests that aren't required and that cover subjects you don't feel confident about.

Determining Which SAT II Tests Are Required

To find out whether the colleges to which you are applying require you to take a particular SAT II test, you'll need to do a bit of research. Call the schools you're interested in, look at college web pages, or talk to your guidance counselor. Often, colleges request that you take the following SAT II tests:

- The Writing SAT II test

- One of the two Math SAT II tests (either Math IC or Math IIC)

- Another SAT II in some other subject of your choice

Not all colleges follow these guidelines, however, so you should take the time to research what tests you need to take in order to apply to the colleges that interest you.

Deciding Which Math SAT II to Take

Few students take both Math SAT II tests, because there really isn't a good reason to take both tests. Instead, you should choose to take one test instead of the other. You should make this choice based on several factors.

1. **Test content.** The two tests cover similar topics, but the Math IIC covers more material than the Math IC does. Level IC covers three years of college-preparatory math: two years of algebra and one year of geometry. Level IIC assumes that in addition to those three years you have also taken a year of trigonometry and/or precalculus.

    Math IC

    Algebra

    Plane geometry (lines and angles, triangles, polygons, circles)

    Solid geometry (cubes, cylinders, cones, spheres, etc.)

    Coordinate geometry (in two dimensions)

    Trigonometry (properties and graphs of sine, cosine, and tangent functions, identities)

    Algebraic functions

    Statistics and sets (distributions, probability, permutations and combinations, groups and sets)

    Miscellaneous topics (logic, series, limits, complex and imaginary numbers)

Math IIC (covers all areas in Math IC with some additional concepts)

Algebra

Plane geometry

Solid geometry

Coordinate geometry (in two and three dimensions, vectors, polar coordinates, parametric equations)

Trigonometry (cosecant, secant, cotangent functions, inverse functions, in non-right triangles)

Statistics and sets

Miscellaneous topics

2. **Question Difficulty.** Not only does the Math IIC cover additional topics, it also covers the basic topics in more difficult ways than the Math IC does.

3. **College Choice.** As you choose between the two tests, keep in mind the specific colleges you're applying to. Colleges with a strong focus on math, such as MIT and Cal Tech, require the Math IIC test. Most other colleges have no such requirement, but some schools may prefer that you take the IIC.

4. **Battle of the Test Curves.** The two tests are scored by very different curves. The Level IIC test is scored on a much more liberal curve: you can miss six or seven questions at the IIC level and still achieve a score of 800. On the IC test, however, you would probably need to answer all the questions correctly to get a perfect score. Here's another example: if you wanted to get a 600 on either test, you would need around 20 correct answers on the IIC test and 33 on the IC test. Some students who have a strong enough math background to take the Math IIC see that the IC is a less difficult test and think that they can get a marvelous score on the IC while their score on the IIC will be only average. But if these students get tripped up by just one or two questions on the Math IC, their scores will not be the impressive showstoppers they might expect.

All in all, if you have the math background to take the Level IIC test, you should go for it. Some students decide to take the Math IC because it's easier, even though they have taken a precalculus course. We don't recommend this plan. True, those students will probably do well on the Math IC test, but colleges will most certainly be more impressed by a student who does fairly well on the SAT II Math IIC than one who does very well on the SAT II Math IC. Also, the friendly curve on the Math IIC means that students who know enough math to take the IIC might very well get a better score on the IIC than they would on the IC.

If after all this you still can't decide which of the two Math SAT IIs to take, try a practice test of each.

Deciding Whether You Should Take an SAT II That Isn't Required

To decide whether you should take a test that isn't required, you have to know two things:

1. What a good score on that SAT II test is

2. Whether you can get that score or higher

Below, we have included a list of the most commonly taken SAT II tests and the average scaled score on each. If you feel confident that you can get a score that is significantly above the average (50 points is significant), taking the test will probably strengthen your college application. Please note that if you are hoping to attend an elite school, you might have to score significantly more than 50 points higher than the national average. The following list is just a general guideline. It's a good idea to call the schools that interest you or to talk to a guidance counselor to get a more precise idea of what score you should be shooting for.

Test	Average Score
Writing	590–600
Literature	590–600
American History	580–590
World History	570–580
Math IC	580–590
Math IIC	655–665
Biology E/M	590–600
Chemistry	605–615
Physics	635–645

As you decide which test to take, be realistic with yourself. Don't just assume you're going to do great without at least taking a practice test and seeing where you stand.

It's a good idea to take three SAT II tests that cover a range of subjects, such as one math SAT II, one humanities SAT II (history or writing), and one science SAT II. But there's no real reason to take *more* than three SAT II tests. Once you've taken the

SAT II tests you need to take, the best way to set yourself apart from other students is to take AP courses and tests. AP tests are harder than the SAT II tests, and as a result, they carry quite a bit more distinction. SAT II tests give you the opportunity to show colleges that you *can* learn and do well when you need to. Taking AP tests shows colleges that you *want* to learn as much as you can.

When to Take an SAT II Subject Test

The best time to take an SAT II Subject Test is right after you've finished a yearlong course in that subject. If, for example, you've finished extensive courses in algebra and geometry by the eleventh grade, then you should take the Math IC test near the end of that year when the subject is still fresh in your mind. (This rule does not apply for the writing, literature, and foreign language SAT II tests; it's best to take those after you've had as much study in the area as possible.)

Unless the colleges to which you are applying use the SAT II for placement purposes, there is no point in taking any SAT II tests after November of your senior year, since you won't get your scores back from ETS until after the college application deadline has passed.

ETS usually sets testing dates for SAT II Subject Tests in October, November, December, January, May, and June. However, not every Subject Test is administered in each of these months. To check when the test you want to take is being offered, visit the College Board website at www.collegeboard.com or do some research in your school's guidance office.

Registering for SAT II Tests

To register for the SAT II test(s) of your choice, you have to fill out some forms and pay a registration fee. We know, we know—it's ridiculous that *you* have to pay for a test that colleges require you to take in order to make *their* jobs easier. But, sadly, there isn't anything we—or you—can do about it. It is acceptable for you to grumble here about the unfairness of the world.

After grumbling, of course, you still have to register. There are two ways to register: online or by mail. To register online, go to www.collegeboard.com. To register by mail, fill out and send in the forms enclosed in the *Registration Bulletin*, which should be available in your high school's guidance office. You can also request a copy of the *Bulletin* by calling the College Board at (609) 771-7600 or writing to:

College Board SAT Program
P.O. Box 6200
Princeton, NJ 08541-6200

You can register to take up to three SAT II tests for any given testing day. Unfortunately, even if you decide to take three tests in one day, you'll still have to pay a separate registration fee for each.

Introduction to the SAT II Math IC

IMAGINE TWO PEOPLE TREKKING THROUGH a jungle toward a magical and therapeutic waterfall. Now, who will reach the soothing waters first, the native to the area, who never stumbles because she knows the placement of every tree and all the twists and turns, or the tourist who keeps falling down and losing his way because he doesn't pay any attention to the terrain? The answer is obvious. Even if the tourist is a little faster, the native will still win, because she knows how to navigate the terrain and turn it to her advantage.

There are no waterfalls or gorgeous jungle scenery on the SAT IIs, but this example illustrates an important point. The structure of the SAT II Math IC is the jungle; taking the test is the challenging trek. Your score is the waterfall.

In this chapter we're going to describe the terrain of the Math IC test. In the following chapter on strategy, we will show you how to navigate and use the terrain to get the best score possible.

Content of the SAT II Math IC

The Math IC test covers a variety of topics in math. ETS, the company that writes the SAT II Math IC, provides the following breakdown of the topics covered in the test:

Topic	Percent of Test	Usual Number of Questions
Algebra	30%	15

Topic	Percent of Test	Usual Number of Questions
Plane Geometry	20%	10
Solid Geometry	6%	3
Coordinate Geometry	12%	6
Trigonometry	8%	4
Functions	12%	6
Statistics and Sets	6%	3
Miscellaneous	6%	3

This breakdown is accurate, but the categories are so broad that the chart won't be much help when you need to focus your studying. That's why we created this more detailed breakdown of the test:

Topic	Percent of Test	Usual Number of Questions
Algebra	30%	15
Arithmetic	1–3%	1
Equation solving	18–22%	10
Binomials, polynomials, quadratics	5–7%	3
Plane Geometry	20%	10
Lines and angles	3–5%	2
Triangles, polygons, circles	14–18%	8
Solid Geometry	6%	3
Solids (cubes, cylinders, cones, etc.)	7–9%	4
Inscribed solids, solids by rotation	1–3%	1
Coordinate Geometry	12%	6
Lines and distance	7–9%	4
Graphing	1–3%	1
Conic sections (parabolas, circles)	3–5%	2
Trigonometry	8%	4
Basic functions (sine, cosine, tangent)	3–5%	2

Topic	Percent of Test	Usual Number of Questions
Trigonometric identities	1–3%	1
Functions	12%	6
Basic, compound, inverse functions	7–9%	4
Graphing functions	1–3%	1
Domain and range of functions	1–3%	2
Statistics and Sets	1–3%	2
Mean, median, mode	6%	3
Probability	1–3%	1
Permutations and combinations	1–2%	0.5
Group questions, sets	1–2%	0.5
Miscellaneous	6%	3
Arithmetic and geometric series	1–2%	0.5
Logic	1–3%	1
Limits	1–2%	0.5
Imaginary numbers	1–2%	0.5

Each question in the practice tests has been categorized according to these categories, so that when you study your practice tests, you can very precisely identify your weaknesses.

Format of the SAT II Math IC

The SAT II Math IC test is a one-hour test made up of 50 multiple-choice questions. The instructions for the test are very simple; you should memorize them so you don't waste time reading them on the day of the test.

> For each of the following problems, decide which is the BEST of the choices given. If the exact numerical value is not one of the choices, select the choice that best approximates this value. Then fill in the corresponding oval on the answer sheet.

Have you read the directions? Have you memorized them? Good. Now for the shocker: the instructions don't cover many of the important aspects of the format and the rules of the test. We're going to remedy that flaw by providing you with a true understanding of the test's format.

- The 50 questions progress in order of difficulty: the easiest questions come first, with the moderately difficult questions in the middle, and the hardest ones last.

- You can skip around while taking the test. The ability to skip the occasional question is helpful, as we will explain in the next chapter.

- All questions are worth the same number of points, whether they are easy or difficult.

All these facts should affect your approach to taking the test, as we will explain in the next chapter on strategy.

The Calculator

Unlike the SAT I, in which a calculator is permitted but not essential to the test, the Math IC test demands the use of a calculator. In fact, that's what the "C" in IC represents. Some questions on the test are specifically designed to test your calculator-using skills.

It is therefore wise to learn all the essentials about calculators before taking the SAT II Math IC. First, make sure you have the right type of calculator. Virtually all calculators are allowed for the test, including the programmable and graphing kind. Laptops, minicomputers, or any machine that prints, makes noise, or needs to be plugged in are not allowed.

Whatever calculator you use for the test should have all the following functions:

- Exponential powers
- Base-10 logarithms
- Sine, cosine, tangent

Make sure you practice performing these functions on the calculator before taking the test. We'll tell you more about how to use calculators for the test in the next chapter.

Scoring the SAT II Math IC

Scoring on the SAT II Math IC is very similar to the scoring for all other SAT II tests. For every right answer, you earn one point. For every wrong answer, you lose $\frac{1}{4}$ of a point. For each question you leave blank, you earn zero points. Add all these points up, and you get your raw score. ETS then converts your raw score to a scaled score according to a special curve. We have included a generalized version of that curve in a table below. Note that the curve changes slightly for each edition of the test, so the table shown will be close to, but not exactly the same as, the table used by the ETS for the particular test you take. You should use this chart to convert your raw scores on practice tests into a scaled score.

Scaled Score	Average Raw Score	Scaled Score	Average Raw Score
800	50	480	18–19
780	49	470	17
770	48	460	16
760	47	450	15
740	46	440	14
730	45	430	13
720	44	430	12
710	43	420	11
700	42	410	10
690	41	400	9
680	40	390	8
670	39	380	7
660	38	370	6
650	37	370	5
640	36	360	4
630	35	350	3
610	34	340	2
600	33	330	1
590	32	330	0
580	31	320	-1
570	30	310	-2
560	29	300	-3
550	28	300	-4
550	27	290	-5
540	26	280	-6
530	25	270	-7
520	24	260	-8
510	23	260	-9
510	22	250	-10
500	21	240	-11
490	20	230	-12

As you can see, this curve is not very forgiving. Getting just one question wrong will lower your score by 20 points. Reiterating what we said in the Introduction to the SAT II Tests, you can miss a bunch of questions on the Math IIC test and still get the same score you would receive on the Math IC test if you missed just one. For example, a raw score of 41 on the Math IIC test receives an equivalent scaled score as a raw score of 49 on the Math IC test.

But not all is hopeless on the SAT II Math IC. On a test of 50 questions, you could score:

- 780 if you answered 49 right, 0 wrong, and left 1 blank

- 740 if you answered 46 right, 0 wrong, and left 4 blank

- 700 if you answered 43 right, 4 wrong, and left 3 blank

- 650 if you answered 39 right, 8 wrong, and left 3 blank

- 650 if you answered 38 right, 4 wrong, and left 7 blank

- 600 if you answered 35 right, 8 wrong, and left 7 blank

These sample scores should suggest that when taking the test you should not imagine your score plummeting with every question you can't confidently answer. So don't get unnecessarily wound up if you run into a difficult question. The key to doing well on the SAT II Math IC is to follow a strategy that ensures you will see and answer all the questions you can answer, while intelligently guessing on those slightly fuzzier questions. We will talk about these strategies in the next chapter.

Strategies for the SAT II Math IC

A MACHINE, NOT A PERSON, WILL SCORE your SAT II Math IC test. The tabulating machine sees only the filled-in ovals on your answer sheet and does not care how you came to these answers; it cares only whether your answers are correct. So whether you knew the right answer because you are a math genius or because you just took a lucky guess, the machine will award you one point. Think of this scoring system as a message to you from the ETS: "We care only about your answers, not about the thought behind them."

So give ETS right answers, as many as possible, using whatever means possible. It's obvious that the SAT II Math IC test allows you to show off your knowledge of math—but the test gives you the same opportunity to show off your fox-like cunning by figuring out what strategies will allow you to best display that knowledge. Remember, the SAT II test is a tool to get into college, so treat it as *your* tool. It wants right answers? Give it right answers, using whatever strategies you can.

Basic Rules of SAT II Test-Taking

There are some rules that apply to all SAT II tests. These rules are so obvious that we hesitate to even call them "strategies." Some of these rules will seem more like common sense to you than anything else. We don't disagree. But it is amazing how a timed test can warp and mangle common sense. So we offer the following list.

Avoid Carelessness

There are two types of carelessness, both of which will cost you points. The first type of carelessness results from moving too fast on the test, whether that speed is caused by overconfidence or frantic fear. By speeding through the test, you make yourself vulnerable to misinterpreting questions, overlooking answer choices, or making logical or mathematical mistakes. As you take the test, make a conscious effort to approach it calmly and to not move so quickly that you become prone to making mistakes.

Whereas the first type of carelessness can be caused by overconfidence, the second type of carelessness results from frustration or lack of confidence. Some students take a defeatist attitude toward tests, assuming they won't be able to answer many of the questions. Such an attitude is a form of carelessness, because it causes the student to ignore reality. Just as the overconfident student assumes she can't be tricked and therefore gets tricked, the student without confidence assumes he can't answer questions and therefore gives up at the first sign of difficulty.

Both kinds of carelessness steal points from you. Avoid them.

Be Careful Gridding Your Answers

The computer that scores SAT II tests is unmerciful. If you answered a question correctly, but somehow made a mistake in marking your answer grid, the computer will mark that question as wrong. If you skipped question 5, but put the answer to question 6 in row 5, and the answer to question 7 in row 6, etc., thereby throwing off your answers for an entire section . . . it will get ugly.

Some test-prep books advise that you should fill in your answer sheet five questions at a time rather than one at a time. Some suggest that you do one question and then fill in the corresponding bubble. We think you should fill out the answer sheet whatever way feels most natural to you; just make sure you're careful while doing it. In our opinion, the best way to ensure that you're being careful is to talk silently to yourself. As you figure out an answer in the test booklet and transfer it over to the answer sheet, say to yourself: "Number 23, B. Number 24, E. Number 25, A."

Know What's in the Reference Area

At the beginning of the SAT II Math IC, there is a reference area that provides you with basic geometric formulas and information.

THE FOLLOWING INFORMATION IS FOR YOUR REFERENCE IN ANSWERING SOME OF THE QUESTIONS IN THIS TEST.

Volume of a right circular cone with radius r and height h: $V = \frac{1}{3}\pi r^2 h$

Lateral area of a right circular cone with circumference of the base c and slant height l: $S = \frac{1}{2}cl$

Volume of a sphere with radius r: $V = \frac{4}{3}\pi r^3$

Surface area of a sphere with radius r: $S = 4\pi r^2$

Volume of a pyramid with base area B and height h: $V = \frac{1}{3}Bh$

You should know all these formulas without needing the reference area; don't neglect to memorize and understand the formulas just because you have the reference area as a crutch. Instead, think of the reference area as a hint to you about what formulas are likely to be needed on the test. If you know those formulas without having to flip back to the reference area, you'll save time, which puts you one step ahead.

Write All Over Your Test Booklet . . .

Draw diagrams or write out equations to help you think. Mark up graphs or charts as necessary. Cross out answers that can't be right. Basically, the test booklet is yours to write all over, and writing can often help clarify things, so that you can work more quickly with fewer mistakes.

. . . But Remember that the SAT Rewards Answers, Not Work

That said, we must qualify our advice. Doing math scratchwork can definitely help you avoid careless errors, but doing pristine work, or more work than necessary, can be more time consuming than it's worth. You must find a balance between speed and accuracy. You need to be able to follow and understand your work, but other people don't. Nobody will look at or reward your work, so don't write it out as if you're being judged.

The Importance of the Order of Difficulty

Imagine that you are taking a test that consists of two questions. After your teacher hands out the test and before you set to work, a helpful little gnome whispers to you, "The first problem is very simple, the second is much harder." Would the gnome's statement affect the way you approach the two problems? The answer, of course, is yes. For a "very simple" question, it seems likely that you should be able to answer it quickly and with little or no agonized second-guessing. You will probably have to spend much more time on a "much harder" question, both to come up with an answer and to check your work to make sure you didn't make an error somewhere along the way.

What about all the other students who didn't hear the gnome? They might labor over the first, easy question, exhaustively checking their work and wasting time that they'll need for the tricky second problem. Then, when those other students do get to the second problem, they might not check their work or be wary of traps, since they have no idea that the problem is so difficult.

The moral here is you should spend less time on the simpler questions that appear early in the test, and devote more time to the harder questions appearing later. Because Math IC questions are ordered by difficulty, it's as if you have that helpful little gnome sitting next to you for the entire test.

Knowing When to Be Wary

Most students answer the easy Math IC questions correctly. Only some students get moderate questions right. Very few students get difficult questions right. What does this mean to you? It means that when you are going through the test, you can often trust your first instincts on an easy question. With difficult questions, however, you should be more cautious. There is a reason most people get these questions wrong: not only are they more difficult and contain more sophisticated mathematical concepts, but they are also often tricky, full of enticing wrong answers that seem as if they must be correct. But because the Math IC orders its questions by difficulty, the test tips you off about when to take a few extra seconds to make sure you haven't been fooled by an answer that only *seems* right.

The tricky answers seem right because they are actually the answers you would get if you were to make a mathematical or logical mistake while working on the problem. For example, let's say you're flying through the test and have to multiply $6 \times 8 \times 3$. So you quickly multiply 6 and 8 to get 42 and then multiply 42 by 3 to get 126. You look down at the answers, and there's 126! That's the answer you came to, and there it is among the answer choices like a little stamp of approval, so you mark it down as your answer and get the question wrong: $6 \times 8 = 48$, not 42, making the correct answer 144.

From this example, you should learn that just because the answer you got is among the answer choices, your answer is not necessarily right. The Math IC is designed to punish those who make careless errors. Don't be one of them. After you get an answer, quickly check your work again.

Math Questions and Time

There are often several ways to answer a Math IC question. You can use trial and error, you can set up and solve an equation, and, for some questions, you might be able to answer the question quickly, intuitively, and elegantly, if you can just spot how to do it. These different approaches to answering questions vary in the amount of time they take. The trial and error method generally takes the longest, while the elegant method of relying on intuitive understanding takes the least amount of time.

Take, for example, the following problem:

Which has a greater area, a square with sides measuring 4 cm or a circle with a radius of the same length?

The most obvious way to solve this problem is simply to plug 4 into the formulas for the area of a square and the area of a circle. Let's do it: Area of a square = s^2, so the area of this square = $4^2 = 16$. Area of a circle = πr^2, and the area of this circle must therefore be $\pi 4^2 = 16\pi$. 16π is obviously bigger than 16, so the circle must be bigger. That worked nicely. But a faster approach would have been to draw a quick to-scale diagram with the square and circle superimposed.

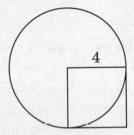

An even quicker way would have been to understand the equations for the area of a square and a circle so well that it was just *obvious* that the circle was bigger, since the equation for the circle will square the 4 and multiply it by π, whereas the equation for the square will only square the 4.

While you may not be able to become a math whiz and just *know* the answer, you can learn to look for a quicker route, such as choosing to draw a diagram instead of working out the equation. And, as with the example above, a quicker route is not necessarily a less accurate one. Making such choices comes down to practice, an awareness that those other routes are out there, and basic mathematical ability.

The value of time-saving strategies is obvious: less time spent on some questions allows you to devote more time to difficult problems. It is this issue of time that separates the students who do terrifically on the Math IC and those who merely do well. Whether or not the ability to find accurate shortcuts is an actual measure of mathematical prowess is not for us to say (though we can think of arguments on either side), but the ability to find those shortcuts absolutely matters on this test.

Shortcuts Are Really Math Intuition

So we've told you all about shortcuts, but now we're going to give you some advice that might seem strange: you shouldn't go into every question searching for a shortcut. If you have to search and search for a shortcut, it might end up taking longer than the typical route. Instead of telling you to seek out math shortcuts, then, we just want you not to get so focused and frantic about getting a question right that you miss the possibility that a shortcut exists. If you go into each question knowing there might be a shortcut and keep your mind open as you think about the question, you have a chance to find the shortcuts you need.

To some extent, you can teach yourself to recognize when a question might contain a shortcut through practice. For example, simply from the problem above, you know that there will probably be a shortcut for all those questions that give you the dimensions of two shapes and ask you to compare them: you can just draw a diagram. A frantic test-taker would see the information given and then seize the simplest route and work out the equations. But if you are a little calmer, you can see that drawing a diagram is the best idea.

Finally, the fact that we advocate using shortcuts doesn't mean you shouldn't focus on learning how to work out problems. In fact, we can guarantee that you're not going to find a shortcut for a problem *unless* you know how to work it out the long way. After all, a shortcut is just you using your knowledge to see a faster way to answer the question. To put it another way, while we've been using the term *math shortcut*, we could just as easily have used the term *math intuition*. If you don't have that knowledge base to work from, you're not going to have anything on which to base your intuition. In contrast, you might be able to figure out an answer by trial and error even if you don't see exactly how to answer the problem.

Making Your Calculator Work for You

As we've already mentioned, the calculator is a very important part of the Math IC test. You need to have the right kind of calculator, be familiar with its operations, and above all, know how to use it intelligently.

There are four types of questions on the test: calculator-friendly, calculator-neutral, calculator-unfriendly, and calculator-useless questions. According to the ETS, about 60 percent of the test falls under the calculator-neutral and -friendly categories. That is, calculators are useful or necessary on 30 of the 50 questions on the SAT II Math IC. The other 20 questions are calculator-unfriendly and -useless. The trick is to be able to identify the different types of questions when presented with them on the test. Here's a breakdown of each of the four types, with examples.

Calculator-Friendly Questions

A calculator is extremely helpful and often necessary to solve calculator-friendly questions. Most likely, problems demanding exact values for exponents, logarithms, or trigonometric functions will need a calculator. Computations that you wouldn't be able to do easily in your head are prime suspects for a calculator. Here's an example:

If $f(x) = \sqrt{x} - 2x^2 + 5$, then what is $f(3.4)$?

(A)   −18.73
(B)   −16.55
(C)   −16.28
(D)   −13.32
(E)   −8.42

This is a simple function question in which you are asked to evaluate $f(x)$ at the value 3.4. All you have to do solve this problem is plug in 3.4 for the variable x and carry out the operations in the function. But unless you know the square root and square of 3.4 off the top of your head, which most test-takers probably wouldn't (and shouldn't), then this problem is extremely difficult to answer without a calculator.

But with a calculator, all you need to do is take the square root of 3.4, subtract twice the square of 3.4, and then add 5. You get answer choice (C), −16.28.

Calculator-Neutral Questions

You have two different choices when faced with a calculator-neutral question. A calculator is useful for these types of problems, but it's probably just as quick and easy to work the problem out by hand.

If $8x = 4^3 \times 2^3$, what is the value of x?

(A)   2
(B)   3
(C)   5
(D)   7
(E)   8

When you see the variable x as a power, you should think of logarithms. A logarithm is the power to which you must raise a given number to equal another number, so in this case, you need to find the exponent x, such that $8^x = 4^3 \times 2^3$. From the definition of logarithms, you know that if given an equation of the form $a^x = b$, then $\log_a b = x$. So you could type in $\log_8 (4^3 \times 2^3)$ on your trusty calculator and find that $x = 3$.

Or, you could recognize that 2 and 4 are both factors of 8, and thinking a step further, that $2^3 = 8$ and $4^3 = 64 = 8^2$. Put together, $4^3 \times 2^3 = 8^2 \times 8 = 8^3$. You come to the same answer that $x = 3$ and that (B) is the right answer.

These two processes take about the same amount of time, so choosing one over the other is more a matter of personal preference than one of strategy. If you feel quite comfortable with your calculator, then you might not want to risk the possibility of making a mental math mistake and should choose the first method. But if you're more prone to error when working with a calculator, then you should choose the second method.

Math IC Strategies

28 • *Making Your Calculator Work for You*

Calculator-Unfriendly Questions

It is possible to answer calculator-unfriendly questions by using a calculator. But while it's possible, it isn't a good idea. These types of problems often have built-in short-cuts—if you know and understand the principle being tested, you can bypass potentially tedious computation with a few simple calculations. Here's a problem that you could solve much more quickly and effectively without the use of a calculator:

$$\frac{\{\cos^2(3 \times 63°) + \sin^2(3 \times 63°)\}^4}{2} =$$

(A) .3261
(B) .5
(C) .6467
(D) .7598
(E) .9238

If you didn't take a moment to think about this problem, you might just rush into it wielding your calculator, calculating the cosine and sine functions, squaring them each and then adding them together, etc. But if you take a closer look, you'll see that $\cos^2(3 \times 63°) + \sin^2(3 \times 63°)$ is a trigonometric identity. More specifically, it is a Pythagorean identity: $\sin^2 q + \cos^2 q = 1$ for any angle q. So, the expression $\{\cos^2(3 \times 63°) + \sin^2(3 \times 63°)\}^4/2$ simplifies to $1^4/2 = 1/2 = .5$. Answer choice (B) is correct.

Calculator-Useless Questions

Even if you wanted to, you wouldn't be able to use your calculator on calculator-useless problems. For the most part, problems involving algebraic manipulation or problems lacking actual numerical values would fall under this category. You should be able to easily identify problems that can't be solved with a calculator. Quite often, the answers for these questions will be variables rather than numbers. Take a look at the following example:

$(x + y - 1)(x + y + 1) =$

(A) $(x + y)^2$
(B) $(x + y)^2 - 1$
(C) $x^2 - y^2$
(D) $x^2 + x - y + y^2 + 1$
(E) $x^2 + y^2 + 1$

This question tests you on an algebraic topic—that is, it asks you how to find the product of two polynomials—and requires knowledge of algebraic principles rather than calculator acumen. You're asked to manipulate variables, not produce a specific value. A calculator would be of no use here.

To solve this problem, you would have to notice that the two polynomials are in the format of a Difference of Two Squares: $(a + b)(a - b) = a^2 - b^2$. In our case, $a = x + y$ and $b = 1$. As a result, $(x + y - 1)(x + y + 1) = (x + y)^2 - 1$. Answer choice (B) is correct.

Don't Immediately Use Your Calculator

The fact that the test contains all four of these question types means that you shouldn't get trigger-happy with your calculator. Just because you've got an awesome shiny hammer doesn't mean you should try to use it to pound in thumbtacks. Using your calculator to try to answer every question on the test would be just as unhelpful.

Instead of reaching instinctively for your calculator, you should come up with a problem-solving plan for each question. Take a brief look at each question so that you understand what it's asking you to do and then decide whether you should use a calculator to solve the problem. That brief instant of time invested in making such decisions will save you a great deal of time later on. For example, what if you came upon the question:

If $(3, y)$ is a point on the graph of $f(x) = \dfrac{x^2 - 5x + 4}{11x - 44}$, then what is y?

(A)   –3
(B)   –1.45
(C)   0
(D)   .182
(E)   4.87

A trigger-happy calculator student might immediately plug in 3 for x. But the student who takes a moment to think about the problem will probably see that the calculation would be much simpler if the function were simplified first. To start, factor 11 out of the denominator:

$$f(x) = \frac{x^2 - 5x + 4}{11x - 44} = \frac{x^2 - 5x + 4}{11(x - 4)}$$

Then, factor the numerator to its simplest form:

$$f(x) = \frac{x^2 - 5x + 4}{11(x - 4)} = \frac{(x - 4)(x - 1)}{11(x - 4)}$$

The $(x - 4)$ cancels out, and the function becomes $f(x) = (x - 1)/11$. At this point you could shift to the calculator and calculate $f(x) = (3 - 1)/11 = {}^2/_{11} = .182$, which is answer (D). If you were very comfortable with math, however, you would see that you don't even have to work out this final calculation. ${}^2/_{11}$ can't work out to any answer other than (D), since you know that ${}^2/_{11}$ isn't negative, zero, or greater than 1.

Approaching Math IC Questions

Though there are four different types of questions on the Math IC, there is a standard procedure that you should use to approach all of them.

1. Read the question without looking at the answers. Determine what the question is asking and come to some conclusion about how to solve it. Do not look at the answers unless you decide that using the process of elimination is the best way to go (we describe how to use the process of elimination below).

2. If you think you can solve the problem, go ahead. Once you've derived an answer, only then see if your answer matches one among the choices.

3. Once you've decided on an answer, test it quickly to make sure it's correct and move on.

Working Backward: The Process of Elimination

If you run into difficulty while trying to solve a multiple-choice problem, you might want to try the process of elimination. For every question, the answer is right in front of you, hidden among five answer choices. So if you can't solve the problem directly, you might be able to plug each answer into the question to see which one works.

Not only can this process help you when you can't figure out a question, there are times when it can actually be faster than setting up an equation, especially if you work strategically. Take the following example:

A classroom contains 31 chairs, some of which have arms and some of which do not. If the room contains 5 more armchairs than chairs without arms, how many armchairs does it contain?

(A)   10
(B)   13
(C)   16
(D)   18
(E)   21

Given this question, you could build the equations:

$$\text{total chairs } (31) = \text{armchairs } (x) + \text{normal chairs } (y)$$
$$\text{normal chairs } (y) = \text{armchairs } (x) - 5$$

Then, since $y = x - 5$, you can make the equation:

$$31 = x + (x - 5)$$
$$31 = 2x - 5$$
$$36 = 2x$$
$$x = 18$$

There are 18 armchairs in the classroom.

This approach of building and working out the equations will produce the right answer, but it takes a long time! What if you strategically plugged in the answers instead? Since the numbers ascend in value, let's choose the one in the middle: (C) 16. This is a smart strategic move because if we plug in 16 and discover that it is too small a number to satisfy the equation, we can eliminate (A) and (B) along with (C). Alternatively, if 16 is too big, we can eliminate (D) and (E) along with (C).

So our strategy is in place. Now let's work it out. If we have 16 armchairs, then we would have 11 normal chairs and the room would contain 27 total chairs. We needed the total numbers of chairs to equal 31, so clearly (C) is not the right answer. But because the total number of chairs is too few, we can also eliminate (A) and (B), the answer choices with smaller numbers of armchairs. If we then plug in (D) 18, we have 13 normal chairs and 31 total chairs. There's our answer. In this instance, plugging in the answers takes less time, and, in general, just seems easier.

Notice that the last sentence began with the words "in this instance." Working backward and plugging in is not always the best method. For some questions it won't be possible to work backward at all. For the test, you will need to build up a sense of when working backward can most help you. A good rule of thumb for deciding whether to work backward is:

> Work backward when the question describes an equation of some sort and the answer choices are all simple numbers.

If the answer choices contain variables, working backward will often be quite difficult; more difficult than working out the problem would be. If the answer choices are complicated, with hard fractions or radicals, plugging in might prove so complex that it's a waste of time.

Substituting Numbers

Substituting numbers is a lot like working backward, except the numbers you plug into the equation *aren't* in the answer choices. Instead, you have to strategically decide on numbers to substitute into the question to take the place of variables.

For example, take the question:

If p and q are odd integers, then which of the following must be odd?

(A) $p + q$
(B) $p - q$
(C) $p^2 + q^2$
(D) $p^2 \times q^2$
(E) $p^2 + q$

It might be hard to conceptualize how the two variables in this problem interact. But what if you chose two odd numbers, let's say 5 and 3, to represent the two variables? Once you begin this substitution it quickly becomes clear that

(A) $p + q = 5 + 3 = 8$
(B) $p - q = 5 - 3 = 2$
(C) $p^2 + q^2 = 25 + 9 = 34$
(D) $p^2 \times q^2 = 25 \times 9 = 225$
(E) $p + q^2 = 5 + 9 = 14$

By picking two numbers that fit the definition of the variables provided by the question, it becomes clear that the answer has to be (D), $p^2 \times q^2$, since it multiplies to 225. (By the way, you could have answered this question without doing the multiplication to 225 since two odd numbers, such as 9 and 25, when multiplied will always result in an odd number.)

Substituting numbers can help you transform problems from the abstract to the concrete. However, you have to remember to keep the substitution consistent. If you're using a 5 to represent p, don't suddenly start using 3. Also, when picking numbers to use as substitutes, pick wisely. Choose numbers that are easy to work with and that fit the definitions provided by the question.

Guessing and the Math IC

Should you guess on the SAT II Math IC? We'll begin to answer this question by posing a question of our own:

> G. O. Metry is holding five cards, numbered 1–5. Without telling you, he has selected one of the numbers as the "correct" card. If you pick a single card, what is the probability that you will choose the correct card?

The answer, of course, is $\frac{1}{5}$. But just as important, you should recognize that the question precisely describes the situation you're in when you blindly guess the answer to any SAT II Math IC question: you have a $\frac{1}{5}$ chance of getting the question right. If you were to guess on 10 questions, you would, according to probability, get two questions right and eight questions wrong.

- Two right answers get you 2 raw points

- Eight wrong answers get you 8 × $-\frac{1}{4}$ points = -2 raw points

Those ten answers, therefore, net you a total of 0 points. Your guessing was a complete waste of time, which is precisely what the ETS wants. They designed the scoring system so that blind guessing is pointless.

Educated Guessing

But what if your guessing isn't blind? Let's revise the earlier question:

If $x + 2x = 6$, what is the value of x?

(A) −2
(B) 2
(C) 3
(D) 0
(E) 1

Let's say you had no idea how to solve this problem, but you did realize that 0 multiplied by any number equals 0, and that $0 + 2 \times 0$ cannot add up to 6. This means that you can eliminate "0" as a possible answer, and now have four choices from which to choose. Is it now worth it to guess? Probability states that if you are guessing between four choices you will get one question right for every three you get wrong. For that one correct answer, you'll get one point, and for the three incorrect answers, you'll lose a total of $\frac{3}{4}$ of a point. $1 - \frac{3}{4} = \frac{1}{4}$, meaning that if you can eliminate even one answer, the odds of guessing turn in your favor: you become more likely to gain points than to lose points.

Therefore, the rule for guessing on the Math IC test is simple: *if you can eliminate even one answer choice on a question, you should definitely guess*. And if you follow the critical-thinking methods we described above about how to eliminate answer choices, you should be able to eliminate at least one answer from almost every question.

Guessing as Partial Credit

Some students feel that guessing is similar to cheating, because by guessing correctly, credit is given where none is due. But instead of looking at guessing as an attempt to gain undeserved points, you should look at it as a form of partial credit. Take the example of the question above. Most people taking the test will see that adding two zeroes will never equal six and will only be able to throw out that choice as a possible answer. But let's say that you also knew that negative numbers added together cannot equal a positive number 6. Don't you deserve something for that extra knowledge? Well, you do get something: when you look at this question, you can throw out both "0" and "−2" as answer choices, leaving you with a $\frac{1}{3}$ chance of getting the question right if you guess. Your extra knowledge gives you better odds of getting this question right, exactly as extra knowledge should.

Pacing

As we said earlier, the questions on the SAT II Math IC test are organized from least to most difficult, with the basic material covered near the beginning and the advanced topics at the end. You always have a sense of what is awaiting you later on in the test. Use this information. Part of your job as you take the test is to make sure you don't spend too much time on the early part of the test. Don't put yourself in the position of having to leave blank those questions near the end of the test that you could have answered *if only you had more time*.

True, answering 50 math questions in 60 minutes is not the easiest of tasks, but if you learn how to pace yourself, you should be able to look at every single question on the test. Note that we said "look at" every question on the test. We didn't say "answer" every question on the test. There is a very big difference between the two.

It is unlikely that you will be able to answer every question on the test. Some questions will stump you, completely resisting your efforts to eliminate even one possible answer choice. Others might demand so much of your time that answering them becomes more trouble than it's worth. While taking five minutes to solve a particularly difficult question might strike you as a moral victory when you're taking the test, it's quite possible that you could have used that same time to answer six other questions that would have vastly increased your score. Instead of getting bogged down on individual questions, you will do better if you learn to skip and leave for later the very difficult questions that you either can't answer or that will take an extremely long time to answer.

By perfecting your pacing on practice tests, you can make sure that you will see every question on the test. And this way, you can select which questions you will and won't answer, rather than running out of time before reaching the end of the test. You're no longer allowing the test to decide, by default, which questions you won't answer.

There are a few simple rules that will make pacing yourself much easier.

- Make sure not to get bogged down on one single question.

- Answer every question to which you know the answer, and make an educated guess for every question in which you can quickly eliminate at least one answer choice.

- Skip questions in which the question and answers refer to concepts completely foreign to you. If you look at the question and answers and have no idea what topics they cover, you have little chance of even coming up with an educated guess. Mark the question in some way to indicate it is very difficult. Return to this type of question only if you have answered everything else. Remember to skip that line in your answer sheet!

Setting a Target Score

You can make the job of pacing yourself easier if you go into the test knowing how many questions you have to answer correctly in order to earn the score that you want. Obviously, you should strive for the best score possible, but be realistic: consider how much you know about math and how well you do in general on SAT-type tests. You should also consider what exactly defines a good score at the colleges where you're applying: is it a 620? A 680? Talk to the admissions offices of the colleges you might want to attend, do a little research in college guidebooks, or talk to your guidance counselor (who will probably advise you to call some admissions offices or to flip through some books). No matter how you do it, you should find out what is the average score of a student going to the schools you want to attend. Take that number and set your target score above it (you want to be *above* average, right?). Then look at the chart we showed you earlier.

You will get:

- 780 if you answered 49 right, 0 wrong, and left 1 blank

- 740 if you answered 46 right, 0 wrong, and left 4 blank

- 700 if you answered 43 right, 4 wrong, and left 3 blank

- 650 if you answered 39 right, 8 wrong, and left 3 blank

- 600 if you answered 35 right, 8 wrong, and left 7 blank

So let's say the average score for the SAT II Math IC for the school you want to attend is a 600. You should set your target at about 650. Looking at this chart, you can see that to get that score, you need to get 39 questions right, can absorb getting 8 wrong, and can leave 3 questions blank.

If you know all these numbers going into the test, you can pace yourself accordingly. You should use practice tests to teach yourself the proper pace, increasing your speed if you find that you aren't getting to answer all the questions you need to or decreasing your pace if you find that you're rushing and making careless mistakes. If you reach your target score during preparation, give yourself a cookie or some other tasty treat and take a break for the day. But just because you hit your target score doesn't mean you should stop working altogether. In fact, you should view reaching your target score as a clue that you can do *better* than that score: set a new target 50-100 points above your original, and work to pick up your pace a little bit and skip fewer questions.

By working to improve your score in small increments, you can slowly work up to top speed, integrating your new knowledge of how to take the test and of the subjects that the test covers without overwhelming yourself by trying to take on too much too soon. If you can handle working just a little faster without becoming careless and losing points, your score will certainly go up. If you meet your new target score, repeat the process.

Practice Tests

Practice Tests Are Your Best Friends

I<small>N THIS CRAZY WORLD OF OURS, THERE IS ONE THING</small> that you can always take for granted: the SAT II Math IC will stay the same. From year to year and test to test, of the 50 questions on the Math IC, 6 or 7 will cover equation solving, 2 to 4 will cover solid geometry, 1 to 3 will cover lines and angles, etc. Obviously, different versions of the SAT II Math IC aren't *exactly* the same. Individual questions will never repeat from test to test. But the subjects that the questions test, and the way in which the questions test those subjects, *will* stay constant.

This constancy can be a great benefit to you as you study for the test. To show how you can use the similarity between different versions of the SAT II Math IC test to your advantage, we provide a case study.

Using the Similarity of the SAT II Math IC for Personal Gain

One day, an eleventh grader named Molly Bloom sits down at the desk in her room and takes a practice test for the SAT II Math IC. Because it makes this example much simpler, let's say she takes the entire test and gets only one question wrong. Molly checks her answers and then jumps from her chair and does a little dance, shimmying to the tune of her own success. After her euphoria passes, she begins to wonder which question she got wrong and returns to her chair. She discovers that the question dealt with parabolas. Looking over the question, Molly at first thinks the test writers made a mistake and that she was right. But at second glance, she realizes that she had misidentified the vertex of the parabola. Molly saw she didn't have a good grasp on how to graph a parabola given its equation so she studies up on her coordinate geometry. She learns the basics of conic sections and *what* causes a parabola's vertex to shift from the origin. All this takes her about ten minutes, after which she vows never to make a mistake on a question involving parabolas.

Analyzing Molly Bloom

Molly's actions seem minor. All she did was study a question she got wrong until she understood why she got it wrong and what she should have done to get it right. But the implications loom large. Molly answered the question incorrectly because she didn't understand the topic it was testing, and the practice test pointed out her shortcoming in the most noticeable way possible: she got the question wrong. After doing her goofy little dance, Molly wasn't content to simply see what the correct answer was and get on with her day. She wanted to see *how* and *why* she got the question wrong and what she should have done or needed to know to get it right. So, with a look of determination and a self-given pep talk, she spent some time studying the question, discovered her mistaken understanding of parabola graphs, and nailed down the ideas behind the material. If Molly were to take that same test again, she definitely would not get that question wrong.

"But she never will take that same test again, so she's never going to see that particular question again," some poor sap who hasn't read this guide might exclaim. "She wasted her time. Wow, Molly Bloom is dumb!"

Why That Poor Sap Really Is a Poor Sap

In some sense, that poor sap is correct: Molly never will take that exact practice test again. But the poor sap is wrong to call Molly derogatory names, because, as we know, the SAT II Math IC is remarkably similar from year to year—both in the topics it covers and in the way it poses questions about those topics. Therefore, when Molly taught herself about conic sections and their graphs, she learned how to answer the similar questions dealing with parabolas and circles that will *undoubtedly* appear on every future practice test and on the real Math IC.

By studying the results of her practice test and figuring out why she got her one question wrong and what she should have known and done to get it right, Molly has targeted a weakness and overcome it.

Molly and You

Molly has it easy. She took a practice test and got only one question wrong. Less than one percent of all people who take the SAT II Math IC will be so lucky. Of course, the only reason Molly got that many right was so that we could use her as an easy example.

So, what if you take a practice test and get 15 questions wrong, and your errors span a number of different math topics? You should do exactly what Molly did. Take your test and *study it*. Identify every question you got wrong, figure out why you got it wrong, and then teach yourself what you should have done to get the question right. If you can't figure out your error, find someone who can.

Think about it. What does an incorrect answer mean? That wrong answer identifies a weakness in your test-taking, whether that weakness is an unfamiliarity with a particular math topic or a tendency to be careless. If you got 15 questions wrong on a practice test, then each of those 15 questions identifies a weakness in your ability to take the SAT II Math IC or your knowledge about the topics tested by the SAT II Math IC. But as you study each question and figure out why you got that question wrong, you are learning how to answer the questions that will appear on the real test. You are discovering your exact math weaknesses and addressing them, and you are learning to understand not just the knowledge behind the question, but the way that ETS asks its questions as well.

If you got 15 questions wrong, it will take a bit more time to study your mistakes. But if you invest that time and study your practice test properly, you will be avoiding future mistakes. Each successive practice test you take should have fewer errors, meaning less time spent studying those errors. More important, you'll be pinpointing what you need to study for the real SAT II Math IC, identifying and overcoming your weaknesses, and learning to answer an increasing variety of questions on the specific topics covered by the test. Taking practice tests and studying them will allow you to teach yourself how to recognize and handle whatever the SAT II Math IC throws at you.

Taking a Practice Test

The example of Miss Molly Bloom shows why studying practice tests can be an extremely powerful study tool. Now we're going to explain how to use that tool.

Controlling Your Environment

Although no one but you ever needs to see your practice-test scores, you should do everything in your power to make the practice test feel like the real SAT II Math IC. The more your practice resembles the real thing, the more helpful it will be. When taking a practice test, follow these rules:

Take the tests timed. Don't give yourself any extra time. Be stricter with yourself than the meanest proctor you can think of would be. Also, don't give yourself time off for bathroom breaks. If you have to go to the bathroom, let the clock keep running; that's what'll happen on the real Math IC.

Take the test in a single sitting. Training yourself to endure an hour of test-taking is part of your preparation.

Find a place to take the test without distractions. Don't take the practice test in a room with lots of people walking through it. Go to a library, your bedroom, an empty class-room—anywhere quiet.

By following these guidelines, you will be more focused while taking the practice test and you will achieve your target score more quickly. However, don't be too discouraged if you find these rules too strict; you can always bend them a little. Preparing for the SAT II should not be so torturous that you don't study! Do whatever you have to do to make yourself study.

Ultimately, if you can follow all of the above rules to the letter, you will probably be better off. But if following those rules makes studying excruciating, find little ways to bend them that won't interfere too much with your concentration.

Practice Test Strategy

You should take the test as if it were the real deal: go for the highest score you can get. This does not mean that you should be more daring than you would be on the actual test, guessing blindly even when you can't eliminate an answer. It doesn't mean that you should carelessly speed through the test. Follow the rules for guessing and for skipping questions that we outlined earlier. The more closely your attitude and strategies during the practice test reflect those you'll employ during the actual test, the more the practice test will accurately predict your strengths and weaknesses: you'll learn what areas you should study and how to pace yourself during the test.

Scoring Your Practice Test

After you take your practice test, you'll want to score it and see how you did. However, when you do your scoring, don't just tally up your raw score. As part of your scoring, you should also keep a list of every question you got wrong and every question you skipped. This list will be your guide when you study your test.

Studying Your ... No, Wait, Go Take a Break

You know how to have fun. Go do that for a while. Come back when you're refreshed.

Studying Your Practice Test

After grading your test, you should have a list of the questions you answered incorrectly or skipped. Studying your test involves using this list and examining each question you answered incorrectly, figuring out why you got the question wrong and understanding what you could have done to get the question right.

Why did you get the question wrong?

There are three reasons why you might have gotten an individual question wrong.

1. You thought you solved the answer correctly, but you actually didn't.

2. You managed to eliminate some answer choices and then guessed among the remaining answers; unfortunately, you guessed wrong.

3. You knew the answer but somehow made a careless mistake.

You should know which of these reasons applies to each question you got wrong.

What could you have done to get the question right?

The reasons you got a question wrong affect how you should think about it while studying your test.

If You Got a Question Wrong for Reason 1—Lack of Knowledge

A question answered incorrectly for Reason 1 identifies a weakness in your knowledge of the math tested on the Math IC test. Discovering this wrong answer gives you an opportunity to target your weakness.

For example, if the question you got wrong refers to factoring quadratics, don't just memorize the roots of certain equations. Learn the fundamental techniques that make different quadratics result in different roots. Remember, you will *not* see a question exactly like the question you got wrong. But you probably *will* see a question that covers the same topic as the practice question. For that reason, when you get a question wrong, don't just figure out the right answer to the question. Study the broader topic that the question tests.

If You Got a Question Wrong for Reason 2—Guessing Wrong

If you guessed wrong, review your guessing strategy. Did you guess smartly? Could you have eliminated more answers? If yes, why didn't you? By thinking in this critical way about the decisions you made while taking the practice test, you can train yourself to make quicker, more decisive, and better decisions.

If you took a guess and chose the incorrect answer, don't let that sour you on guessing. Even as you go over the question and figure out if there were any ways for you to have answered the question without having to guess, remind yourself that if you eliminated at least one answer, you followed the right strategy even if you got the question wrong.

If You Got a Question Wrong for Reason 3—Carelessness

If you discover you got a question wrong because you were careless, it might be tempting to say to yourself, "Oh, I made a careless error," and assure yourself you won't do that again. That is not enough. You made that careless mistake for a reason, and you should try to figure out why. Whereas getting a question wrong because you didn't know the answer constitutes a weakness in your knowledge about the test, making a careless mistake represents a weakness in your *method of taking the test*.

To overcome this weakness, you need to approach it in the same critical way you would approach a lack of knowledge. Study your mistake. Reenact your thought process on the problem and see where and how your carelessness came about: were you rushing? Did you jump at the first answer that seemed right instead of reading all the answers? Know your error and look it in the eye. If you learn precisely what your mistake was, you are much less likely to make that mistake again.

If You Left the Question Blank

It is also a good idea to study the questions you left blank on the test, since those questions constitute a reservoir of lost points.

A blank answer is a result either of:

1. A total inability to answer a question

2. A lack of time

In the case of the first possibility, you should see if there were some way you might have been able to eliminate an answer choice or two and put yourself in a better position to guess. In the second case, look over the question and see whether you think you could have answered it. If you could have, then you know that you are throwing away points and probably working too slowly. If you couldn't, then carry out the steps above: study the relevant material and review your guessing strategy.

The Secret Weapon: Talking to Yourself

Yeah, it's embarrassing. Yeah, you'll look silly. But other than physical violence, talking to yourself is perhaps the best way to pound something into your brain. As you go through the steps of studying a question, you should talk them out. When you verbalize something to yourself, it makes it much harder to delude yourself into thinking that you're working if you're really not.

SAT II Math IC
Practice Test 1

MATH IC TEST 1 ANSWER SHEET

1. Ⓐ Ⓑ Ⓒ Ⓓ Ⓔ	18. Ⓐ Ⓑ Ⓒ Ⓓ Ⓔ	35. Ⓐ Ⓑ Ⓒ Ⓓ Ⓔ
2. Ⓐ Ⓑ Ⓒ Ⓓ Ⓔ	19. Ⓐ Ⓑ Ⓒ Ⓓ Ⓔ	36. Ⓐ Ⓑ Ⓒ Ⓓ Ⓔ
3. Ⓐ Ⓑ Ⓒ Ⓓ Ⓔ	20. Ⓐ Ⓑ Ⓒ Ⓓ Ⓔ	37. Ⓐ Ⓑ Ⓒ Ⓓ Ⓔ
4. Ⓐ Ⓑ Ⓒ Ⓓ Ⓔ	21. Ⓐ Ⓑ Ⓒ Ⓓ Ⓔ	38. Ⓐ Ⓑ Ⓒ Ⓓ Ⓔ
5. Ⓐ Ⓑ Ⓒ Ⓓ Ⓔ	22. Ⓐ Ⓑ Ⓒ Ⓓ Ⓔ	39. Ⓐ Ⓑ Ⓒ Ⓓ Ⓔ
6. Ⓐ Ⓑ Ⓒ Ⓓ Ⓔ	23. Ⓐ Ⓑ Ⓒ Ⓓ Ⓔ	40. Ⓐ Ⓑ Ⓒ Ⓓ Ⓔ
7. Ⓐ Ⓑ Ⓒ Ⓓ Ⓔ	24. Ⓐ Ⓑ Ⓒ Ⓓ Ⓔ	41. Ⓐ Ⓑ Ⓒ Ⓓ Ⓔ
8. Ⓐ Ⓑ Ⓒ Ⓓ Ⓔ	25. Ⓐ Ⓑ Ⓒ Ⓓ Ⓔ	42. Ⓐ Ⓑ Ⓒ Ⓓ Ⓔ
9. Ⓐ Ⓑ Ⓒ Ⓓ Ⓔ	26. Ⓐ Ⓑ Ⓒ Ⓓ Ⓔ	43. Ⓐ Ⓑ Ⓒ Ⓓ Ⓔ
10. Ⓐ Ⓑ Ⓒ Ⓓ Ⓔ	27. Ⓐ Ⓑ Ⓒ Ⓓ Ⓔ	44. Ⓐ Ⓑ Ⓒ Ⓓ Ⓔ
11. Ⓐ Ⓑ Ⓒ Ⓓ Ⓔ	28. Ⓐ Ⓑ Ⓒ Ⓓ Ⓔ	45. Ⓐ Ⓑ Ⓒ Ⓓ Ⓔ
12. Ⓐ Ⓑ Ⓒ Ⓓ Ⓔ	29. Ⓐ Ⓑ Ⓒ Ⓓ Ⓔ	46. Ⓐ Ⓑ Ⓒ Ⓓ Ⓔ
13. Ⓐ Ⓑ Ⓒ Ⓓ Ⓔ	30. Ⓐ Ⓑ Ⓒ Ⓓ Ⓔ	47. Ⓐ Ⓑ Ⓒ Ⓓ Ⓔ
14. Ⓐ Ⓑ Ⓒ Ⓓ Ⓔ	31. Ⓐ Ⓑ Ⓒ Ⓓ Ⓔ	48. Ⓐ Ⓑ Ⓒ Ⓓ Ⓔ
15. Ⓐ Ⓑ Ⓒ Ⓓ Ⓔ	32. Ⓐ Ⓑ Ⓒ Ⓓ Ⓔ	49. Ⓐ Ⓑ Ⓒ Ⓓ Ⓔ
16. Ⓐ Ⓑ Ⓒ Ⓓ Ⓔ	33. Ⓐ Ⓑ Ⓒ Ⓓ Ⓔ	50. Ⓐ Ⓑ Ⓒ Ⓓ Ⓔ
17. Ⓐ Ⓑ Ⓒ Ⓓ Ⓔ	34. Ⓐ Ⓑ Ⓒ Ⓓ Ⓔ	

REFERENCE INFORMATION

THE FOLLOWING INFORMATION IS FOR YOUR REFERENCE IN ANSWERING SOME OF THE QUESTIONS IN THIS TEST:

Volume of a right circular cone with radius r and height h: $V = \frac{1}{3}\pi r^2 h$

Lateral area of a right circular cone with circumference of the base c and slaight height ℓ: $S = \frac{1}{2}c\ell$

Volume of a sphere with radius r: $V = \frac{4}{3}\pi r^3$

Surface area of a sphere with radius r: $S = 4\pi r^2$

Volume of a pyramid with base area B and height h: $V = \frac{1}{3}Bh$

MATHEMATICS LEVEL IC TEST

For each of the following problems, decide which is the BEST of the choices given. If the exact numerical value is not one of the choices, select the choice that best approximates this value. Then fill in the corresponding oval on the answer sheet.

<u>Notes:</u> (1) A calculator will be necessary for answering some (but not all) of the questions in this test. For each question you will have to decide whether or not you should use a calcuator. The calculator you use must be at least a scientific calculator; programmable calculators and calculators that can display graphs are permitted.

(2) For some questions in this test you may need to decide whether your calculator should be in radian or degree mode.

(3) Figures that accompany problems in this test are intended to provide information useful in solving the problems. They are drawn as accurately as possible EXCEPT when it is stated in a specific problem that its figure is not drawn to scale. All figures lie in a plane unless otherwise indicated.

(4) Unless otherwise specified, the domain of any function f is assumed to be the set of all real numbers x for which $f(x)$ is a real number.

(5) Reference information that may be useful in answering the questions in this test can be found on the page preceding Question 1.

USE THIS SPACE FOR SCRATCHWORK.

1. If $\dfrac{3}{z-2} = \dfrac{4}{z+1}$, then $z =$

(A) 9
(B) 10
(C) 11
(D) 12
(E) 13

2. If $y = (7-b)^3$ and $b = 5$, then $y =$

(A) 1
(B) 2
(C) 4
(D) 8
(E) 16

3. What is the least positive integer that is divisible by 2, 5, and 6 ?

(A) 90
(B) 75
(C) 60
(D) 45
(E) 30

GO ON TO THE NEXT PAGE

4. In Figure 1, if the area of $\triangle ABC$ is 9, then $m =$

    (A) 1
    (B) 2
    (C) 3
    (D) 4
    (E) 5

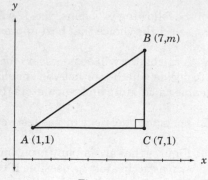

Figure 1

5. What is the equation of the line that passes through the point $(\frac{1}{2}, \frac{2}{3})$ and is perpendicular to the line $y = -\frac{1}{3}x + 1$?

    (A) $y - \frac{1}{2} = 3\left(x - \frac{2}{3}\right)$

    (B) $y - \frac{2}{3} = 3\left(x - \frac{1}{2}\right)$

    (C) $y + \frac{2}{3} = 3\left(x - \frac{1}{2}\right)$

    (D) $y - \frac{2}{3} = \frac{1}{3}\left(x - \frac{1}{2}\right)$

    (E) $y + \frac{2}{3} = \frac{1}{3}\left(x + \frac{1}{2}\right)$

6. $\dfrac{2^2 - 1}{2 - 1} + \dfrac{3^2 - 1}{3 - 1} + \dfrac{4^2 - 1}{4 - 1} + \dfrac{5^2 - 1}{5 - 1} =$

    (A) 18
    (B) 20
    (C) 22
    (D) 24
    (E) 26

7. If $x^2 - y^2 = 15$ and $x + y = 5$, then $xy =$

    (A) 10
    (B) 7
    (C) 5.5
    (D) 5
    (E) 4

8. If $\sqrt[3]{t} = 2$, then $\dfrac{t^2}{10} =$

    (A) 8.2
    (B) 6.4
    (C) 3.2
    (D) 0.32
    (E) 0.16

GO ON TO THE NEXT PAGE

USE THIS SPACE FOR SCRATCHWORK.

9. The cube in Figure 2 consists of 64 small cubes. If the outside of the larger cube is painted red, then what percentage of the smaller cubes will not have paint on any of their faces?

(A) 12.5%
(B) 14.7%
(C) 35%
(D) 50%
(E) 87.5%

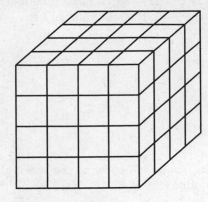

Figure 2

10. A circle of radius 5 rolls a distance of 250π. How many complete revolutions does the circle make?

(A) 17
(B) 21
(C) 23
(D) 25
(E) 32

11. The distance between the points $(2, -5)$ and $(6, 12)$ is approximately

(A) 8.06
(B) 10.63
(C) 12.12
(D) 14.85
(E) 17.46

12. John is four times older than Mary. Mary is three years younger than Sam. If three years ago Sam was twice as old as Mary was, then how old is John now?

(A) 48
(B) 36
(C) 24
(D) 23
(E) 18

13. If $24^{j/3} = 2^5 \cdot 3^5 \cdot 4^5$, then $j =$

(A) 10
(B) 15
(C) 25
(D) 35
(E) 50

GO ON TO THE NEXT PAGE

14. If $p(x) = x^3 + 2x^2 + kx + 4$ has a remainder of 24 when it is divided by $x - 2$, then the value of k is

   (A) 1
   (B) 2
   (C) 3
   (D) 4
   (E) 5

15. An operation is defined for all positive real numbers x and y by the equation $x \lozenge y = x^y - y^x$. If $2 \lozenge s = 0$, then s could equal

   I.   2
   II. 3
   III. 4

   (A) I only
   (B) III only
   (C) I and III only
   (D) II and III only
   (E) I, II, and III

16. George spent the day shopping and eating in restaurants. He spent $\frac{2}{5}$ of his money on food, $\frac{1}{6}$ of his money on books, and the remainder of his money on a leather jacket. If the jacket cost $104, then how much did George spend on books?

   (A) $33.33
   (B) $36.00
   (C) $39.00
   (D) $40.00
   (E) $96.00

17. $||-x| - |2x|| - ||x| - |4x|| =$

   (A) $-2x$
   (B) $-x$
   (C) 0
   (D) x
   (E) $2x$

GO ON TO THE NEXT PAGE

USE THIS SPACE FOR SCRATCHWORK.

18. In Figure 3, lines l and m are parallel. Lines s and t are transverse and intersect at point P. If $\angle x = 85°$ and $\angle y = 120°$, then $\angle \theta =$

   (A) 75°
   (B) 65°
   (C) 45°
   (D) 35°
   (E) 30°

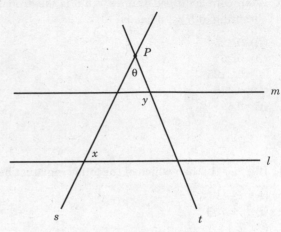

Note: Figure not drawn to scale.

Figure 3

19. In Figure 4, a quadrilateral $ABOC$ is inscribed within a circle with center O. If $\angle x = 20°$ and the circle has radius 2.5, then what is the approximate length of arc $\overset{\frown}{BPC}$?

   (A) 0.44
   (B) 0.87
   (C) 1.31
   (D) 1.40
   (E) 1.75

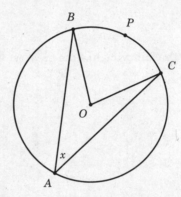

Note: Figure not drawn to scale.

Figure 4

20. The fourth root of the cube of a number is 8. What is the number?

   (A) 8
   (B) 16
   (C) 32
   (D) 64
   (E) 128

21. If $g(x) = \dfrac{x}{\sqrt{x-1}}$ for $x > 1$, then $g(10) =$

   (A) 10

   (B) 5

   (C) $\dfrac{10}{3}$

   (D) 3

   (E) $\dfrac{3}{2}$

22. What are all values of b for which $|7 - b| > 5$?

   (A) $b < 2$
   (B) $b > 12$
   (C) $2 < b < 12$
   (D) $b < 2$ or $b > 12$
   (E) $-12 < b < -2$

GO ON TO THE NEXT PAGE

USE THIS SPACE FOR SCRATCHWORK.

23. A fair coin is flipped 4 times. What is the probability of obtaining at least 3 heads?

(A) 0.125
(B) 0.25
(C) 0.3125
(D) 0.375
(E) 0.5

24. If $i = \sqrt{-1}$, then which of the following must be equal to zero?

(A) $i + i^4$
(B) $i^3 - i^{12}$
(C) $i^{15} + i^{19}$
(D) $i^{21} + i^{25}$
(E) $i^{25} + i^{31}$

25. Which of the following has the greatest value?

(A) 2^{201}
(B) 4^{100}
(C) 8^{70}
(D) 16^{50}
(E) 32^{39}

26. In Figure 5, if $\theta_1 = \frac{\theta_2}{2}$, then what is the value of a?

(A) 12.12
(B) 10.10
(C) 6.06
(D) 4.04
(E) 3.5

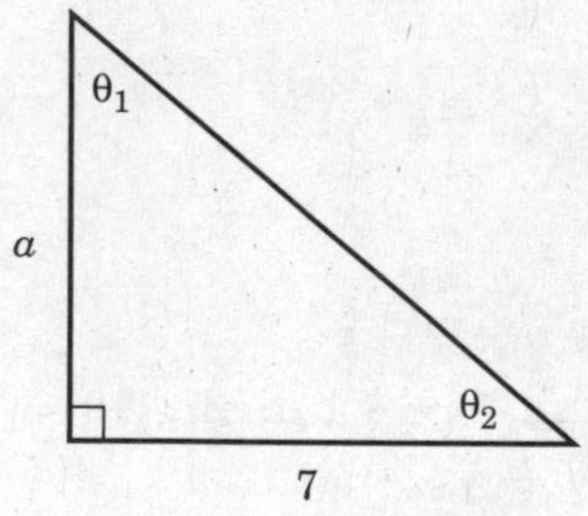

Note: Figure not drawn to scale.

Figure 5

27. An equation for the circle that has its center at the origin and passes through the point (1, 6) is

(A) $x^2 + y^2 = \sqrt{7}$
(B) $x^2 + y^2 = 7$
(C) $x^2 + y^2 = \sqrt{37}$
(D) $x^2 + y^2 = 37$
(E) $x^2 + y^2 = 49$

GO ON TO THE NEXT PAGE

USE THIS SPACE FOR SCRATCHWORK.

28. If m and n are positive odd integers, which of the following must be even?

   I. $\dfrac{m+n}{2}$

   II. $m^n + 1$

   III. $m^2 + n^2 + 1$

   (A) I only
   (B) II only
   (C) II and III
   (D) I, II, and III
   (E) None of the above

29. The value of $(1 + \cos\theta)^2 - 2\cos\theta + \sin^2\theta$ is

   (A) 2
   (B) 0
   (C) $\cos\theta$
   (D) $\sin^2\theta$
   (E) 1

30. The heights of 5 people were measured and the average (arithmetic mean) was calculated to be 70 inches. Of these 5 people, the heights of 3 of them were equal to the median height. If the median height was 68 inches, then which of the following <u>must</u> be true?

   (A) The tallest person was 70 inches.
   (B) The shortest person was shorter than 68 inches.
   (C) At least two people were taller than the median height.
   (D) The height of the tallest person was above 70 inches.
   (E) At least one person was shorter than 68 inches.

31. If $h(x) = 3 - 4x$ for all x, then the slope of the line given by $y = h\left(\dfrac{x}{2} + 2\right)$ is

   (A) 8
   (B) 4
   (C) 2
   (D) 0
   (E) −2

GO ON TO THE NEXT PAGE

32. Which of the following <u>cannot</u> be the result of the intersection of a plane and a cylinder?

    (A) A point
    (B) A line
    (C) A triangle
    (D) A rectangle
    (E) An ellipse

33. The surface area of a cube is numerically equal to its volume. What is the length of a side of the cube?

    (A) 6
    (B) 5
    (C) 4
    (D) 3
    (E) $\sqrt{6}$

34. For which of the following quadratic equations is the sum of its roots equal to 6 and the product of its roots equal to 7?

    (A) $x^2 + 6x - 7 = 0$
    (B) $x^2 + 6x + 7 = 0$
    (C) $2x^2 - 6x + 7 = 0$
    (D) $2x^2 - 12x + 14 = 0$
    (E) $2x^2 - 12x - 14 = 0$

35. In Figure 6, $AB \parallel DE$. If $CE = 5$ and $CB = 7$, then what is the value of $\dfrac{x}{y}$?

    (A) 3
    (B) 2.5
    (C) 2
    (D) 1.4
    (E) 0.4

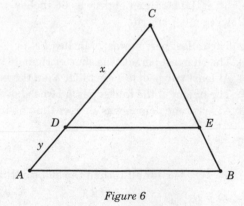

Figure 6

GO ON TO THE NEXT PAGE

36. In Figure 7, if $\triangle PQR$ is first reflected across the x-axis and then relected across the y-axis, which of the following will be the coordinates of the point Q?

(A) $(1,-3)$
(B) $(2,-3)$
(C) $(1,3)$
(D) $(-1,3)$
(E) $(-1,-3)$

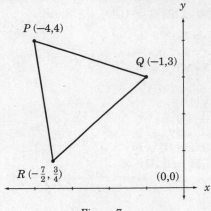

Figure 7

37. How many 4-digit odd numbers are there between 1000 and 3999, inclusive?

(A) 3000
(B) 1500
(C) 1499
(D) 1000
(E) 750

38. In 2002, the value of a car was $5450. If the resale value of the car depreciates at a rate of 7% each year, what will the value of the car be in 2010?

(A) $4012.45
(B) $3545.50
(C) $3441.12
(D) $3279.27
(E) $3049.72

39. If $0° < \theta < 90°$, $x \neq y$, $x > 0$, $y > 0$, and $\cos(\theta) = \dfrac{x}{y}$, then $\sin(\theta) =$

(A) $\dfrac{y}{x}$

(B) $\dfrac{y}{\sqrt{y^2 - x^2}}$

(C) $\dfrac{\sqrt{x^2 - y^2}}{y}$

(D) $\dfrac{\sqrt{y^2 - x^2}}{y}$

(E) $\dfrac{\sqrt{y^2 - x^2}}{x}$

GO ON TO THE NEXT PAGE

USE THIS SPACE FOR SCRATCHWORK.

40. If $f(x) = ax + b$ and $f(f(x)) = x$ for all x, then which of the following __must__ be true?

    I. $b = 1$
    II. $a = 1$ or $a = -1$
    III. $b = 0$ if $a = 1$

    (A) I only
    (B) II only
    (C) III only
    (D) II and III only
    (E) I, II, and III

41. In Figure 8, if a right circular cone is inscribed within a cube whose volume is 125, then the volume of the cone is approximately

    (A) 98.17
    (B) 78.54
    (C) 66.12
    (D) 45.45
    (E) 32.72

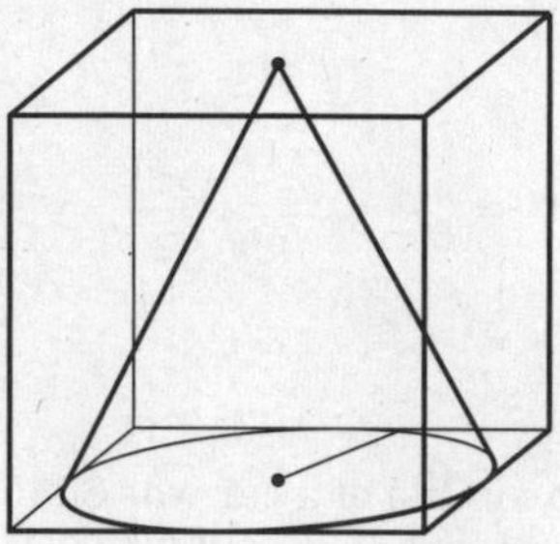

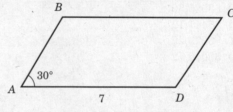

Figure 8

42. In Figure 9, the area of parallelogram $ABCD$ is 42. What is the perimeter of the parallelogram?

    (A) 19
    (B) 25
    (C) 28
    (D) 33.33
    (E) 38

Note: Figure not drawn to scale.
Figure 9

43. What is the range of the function g, where $g(x) = 1 - (2 - x)^2$ is defined for $1 \le x \le 4$?

    (A) $-3 \le g(x) \le 0$
    (B) $-3 \le g(x) \le 2$
    (C) $-3 \le g(x) \le 1$
    (D) $-1 \le g(x) \le 3$
    (E) $-2 \le g(x) \le 3$

GO ON TO THE NEXT PAGE

44. The n-th term in the sequence of numbers $\{2, 5, 10, 17, ...\}$ can be determined by which of the following?

    (A) $5n - 3$
    (B) $2 + 3(n - 1)$
    (C) $3n - 1$
    (D) $n^2 + 1$
    (E) $n^2 - 1$

45. If the line $y = x + b$ is tangent to the circle defined by $x^2 + y^2 = 100$, then b equals

    (A) 10
    (B) 10 or -10
    (C) $10\sqrt{2}$ or $-10\sqrt{2}$
    (D) $10\sqrt{2}$
    (E) $10\sqrt{3}$ or $-10\sqrt{3}$

46. For which of the following is $f(x) = f(-x)$?

    I. $f(x) = |4 - x^2|$
    II. $f(x) = \dfrac{1}{x^3}$
    III. $f(x) = \dfrac{1}{1 + x^2}$

    (A) I only
    (B) III only
    (C) I and II only
    (D) I and III only
    (E) I, II, and III

47. In Figure 10, the radius of circle O is 5. If the length of chord AB is 5, then the area of the shaded region is approximately

    (A) 15.35
    (B) 14.35
    (C) 12.35
    (D) 8.35
    (E) 2.26

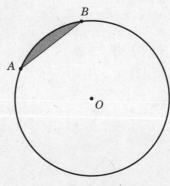

Figure 10

GO ON TO THE NEXT PAGE

48. How many milliliters (ml) of pure alcohol must be added to 75 milliliters of a 20% alcohol solution (by volume) so that the resulting solution is 40% alcohol?

   (A) 15 ml
   (B) 25 ml
   (C) 30 ml
   (D) 35 ml
   (E) 45 ml

49. If $f(x) = x^2 - 12x + 35$ and $g(x) = -x^2 + 4x + 21$, then for all x such that $x \neq -3$ or $x \neq 7$, $\dfrac{f(x)}{g(x)} =$

   (A) $\dfrac{x+5}{x+3}$

   (B) $\dfrac{x-5}{x+3}$

   (C) $\dfrac{5-x}{x+3}$

   (D) $\dfrac{5-x}{x-3}$

   (E) $\dfrac{x-5}{x-3}$

50. "If p, then not q" is logically equivalent to which of the following?

   (A) If q, then not p
   (B) If q, then p
   (C) If not q, then p
   (D) If p, then q
   (E) If not q, then not p

S T O P

IF YOU FINISH BEFORE TIME IS CALLED, YOU MAY CHECK YOUR WORK ON THIS TEST ONLY.
DO NOT TURN TO ANY OTHER TEST IN THIS BOOK.

SAT II Math IC
Practice Test 1
Explanations

Calculating Your Score

Question Number	Correct Answer	Right	Wrong	Question Number	Correct Answer	Right	Wrong	Question Number	Correct Answer	Right	Wrong
1.	C	___	___	18.	D	___	___	35.	B	___	___
2.	D	___	___	19.	E	___	___	36.	A	___	___
3.	E	___	___	20.	B	___	___	37.	B	___	___
4.	D	___	___	21.	C	___	___	38.	E	___	___
5.	B	___	___	22.	D	___	___	39.	D	___	___
6.	A	___	___	23.	C	___	___	40.	D	___	___
7.	E	___	___	24.	E	___	___	41.	E	___	___
8.	B	___	___	25.	C	___	___	42.	E	___	___
9.	A	___	___	26.	A	___	___	43.	C	___	___
10.	D	___	___	27.	D	___	___	44.	D	___	___
11.	E	___	___	28.	B	___	___	45.	C	___	___
12.	C	___	___	29.	A	___	___	46.	D	___	___
13.	B	___	___	30.	D	___	___	47.	E	___	___
14.	B	___	___	31.	E	___	___	48.	B	___	___
15.	C	___	___	32.	C	___	___	49.	C	___	___
16.	D	___	___	33.	A	___	___	50.	A	___	___
17.	A	___	___	34.	D	___	___				

Your raw score for the SAT II Math IC test is calculated from the number of questions you answer correctly and incorrectly. Once you have determined your composite score, use the conversion table on page 18 of this book to calculate your scaled score. To calculate your raw score, count the number of questions you answered correctly: _____

A

Count the number of questions you answered incorrectly, and multiply that number by $\frac{1}{4}$:

$$ \underline{\hspace{3cm}} \times \frac{1}{4} = \underline{\hspace{3cm}} $$
B C

Subtract the value in field C from value in field A: _____
D

Round the number in field D to the nearest whole number. This is your raw score: _____
E

Math IC Test 1 Explanations

1. **(C)** *Algebra: Equation Solving*

Cross multiply the terms $z - 2$ and $z + 1$ to solve for z.

$$\frac{3}{z-2} = \frac{4}{z+1}$$

$$3(z + 1) = 4(z - 2)$$

$$3z + 3 = 4z - 8$$

$$z = 11$$

2. **(D)** *Algebra: Equation Solving*

Simply plug in 5 for b and then carry out the specified operations.

$$y = (7 - 5)^3$$

$$= (2)^3$$

$$= 8$$

3. **(E)** *Fundamentals: Integers*

The correct answer is the smallest number divisible by 2, 5, and 6. There are two methods of approaching this problem. The first is to determine the Least Common Multiple (LCM) of 2, 5, and 6. Since 2 and 5 are both prime numbers, you know that 2 and 5 must be factors of the LCM. As 6 is divisible by both 2 and 3, you know that 3 must also be a factor of the LCM. Therefore, the LCM of 2, 5, and 6 is $2 \cdot 3 \cdot 5 = 30$.

The second method is simply to divide each of the answer choices by 2, 5, and 6; see which of the answer choices is evenly divisible by all three numbers; then choose the smallest. Since the answer choices are listed from largest to smallest, it would be most efficient to start with the last, or smallest, one.

4. **(D)** *Plane Geometry: Triangles; Coordinate Geometry: Lines and Distance*

The area of any triangle is given by $\frac{1}{2} \cdot Base \cdot Height$. Since $\triangle ABC$ is a right triangle, the base and height are easy to find. Use the x-coordinates of points A and C to determine that the length of side $AC = 7 - 1 = 6$, and use the y-coordinates of points C and B to determine that the length of side $CB = m - 1$. Now plug these values into the area formula.

$$\frac{1}{2} \cdot Base \cdot Height = \frac{1}{2} \cdot AC \cdot CB$$

$$= \frac{1}{2} \cdot 6 \cdot (m - 1)$$

$$= 3m - 3$$

The question tells you that the area of the triangle is 9, so you can now find m by setting the above expression equal to 9:

$$9 = 3m - 3$$

$$12 = 3m$$

$$4 = m$$

5. (B) *Coordinate Geometry: Lines and Slope*

From the answer choices, you can see that you're looking for an equation written in the point-slope formula, $y - y_1 = m_\perp (x - x_1)$, where $m_\perp$ is the slope of the line perpendicular to $y = -\frac{1}{3}x + 1$. The line $y = -\frac{1}{3}x + 1$ has a slope of $m = -\frac{1}{3}$. The slope of a perpendicular line must be $m_\perp = -\frac{1}{m}$, so you're looking for a line with a slope $m = 3$. Since the lines in (D) and (E) have slopes equal to $\frac{1}{3}$, you can rule those answers out. Plug $\left(\frac{1}{2}, \frac{2}{3}\right) = (x_1, y_1)$ and $m = 3$ into the point-slope formula to get $y - \frac{2}{3} = 3\left(x - \frac{1}{2}\right)$, or answer choice (B).

6. (A) *Algebra: Writing Equations, Exponents*

You could use a calculator to work out the answer to this question, but it would take quite a bit of time. This question is easier to solve by hand, if you can spot its pattern.

$$\frac{2^2 - 1}{2 - 1} = 3$$

$$\frac{3^2 - 1}{3 - 1} = 4$$

In general, the following rule works:

$$\frac{n^2 - 1}{n - 1} = \frac{(n - 1)(n + 1)}{n - 1}$$

$$= n + 1$$

Applying this rule, you can reduce the problem to $3 + 4 + 5 + 6 = 18$.

7. (E) *Algebra: Polynomials*

Whenever you see $x^2 - y^2$, you should immediately factor it as $(x + y)(x - y)$, since it's a difference of squares. On the Math IC, this rewriting will almost always reveal a simple solution to the problem.

$$x^2 - y^2 = 15$$
$$(x + y)(x - y) = 15$$

Now you can substitute 5 for $x + y$:

$$5(x - y) = 15$$

$x - y$ must equal 3. Now write the equations one on top of the other, and add them.

$$x + y = 5$$
$$x - y = 3$$

Adding these two equations will cancel the y's, and you'll have:

$$2x = 8$$
$$x = 4$$

If $x = 4$, then $y = 1$ and $xy = 4$.

8. **(B)** *Algebra: Equation Solving*

Since you are given $\sqrt[3]{t} = 2$, you can solve for t and then substitute the answer into $\frac{t^2}{10}$.

$$\sqrt[3]{t} = 2$$
$$t = 8$$

Plug this value into the second equation $\frac{t^2}{10}$:

$$\frac{8^2}{10} = \frac{64}{10}$$
$$= 6.4$$

9. **(A)** *Solid Geometry: Prisms*

The larger cube consists of 64 smaller cubes, and you can see from the figure that each side of the larger cube is 4 small cubes in length. When the outside of the larger cube is painted, every small cube that has at least one side facing out will be painted. To find the number of cubes without any paint, you simply strip off this outer layer of small painted cubes, as in the figure below:

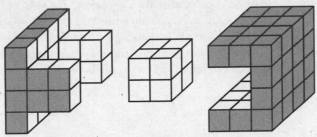

You can see that there are 8 smaller cubes untouched by paint. The percentage of the unpainted smaller cubes is $\frac{8}{64} = 0.125$, or 12.5%.

10. **(D)** *Plane Geometry: Circles*

This question asks you to figure out how many revolutions a circle makes when it travels a certain distance, and it gives you the radius of the circle and the distance the circle rolls. You need to figure out how to relate the circle's radius to the distance traveled. The solution is to use the radius to find the circumference of the circle. When a circle completes one revolution, it has traveled a distance equal to its own circumference. (If you're having trouble grasping this idea, picture a circle rolling out into a line; the length of that line is equal to the circumference of the circle. When you reach the end of the line, you have completed a full turn around the circle.) In order to find how many revolutions the circle makes, you need to divide the total distance traveled by the distance traveled in one revolution (i.e. the circumference of the circle). You know the formula for a circle's circumference is $2\pi r$, so plug in 5 for the radius and find that the circumference is 10π. Now divide 250π by the circumference to find the number of revolutions:

$$\frac{250\pi}{10\pi} = 25 \text{ revolutions}$$

11. **(E)** *Coordinate Geometry: Lines and Distance*

This question calls for a straightforward application of the distance formula, which you definitely should memorize for the Math IC. The formula for the distance d between two points (x_1, y_1) and (x_2, y_2) in a plane is:

$$
\begin{aligned}
d &= \sqrt{(x_1 - x_2)^2 + (y_1 - y_2)^2} \\
&= \sqrt{(2-6)^2 + (-5-12)^2} \\
&= \sqrt{(-4)^2 + (-17)^2} \\
&= \sqrt{16 + 289} \\
&= \sqrt{305} \\
&= 17.46
\end{aligned}
$$

12. **(C)** *Algebra: Writing Equations, Word Problems*

This question gives you the relationships among the ages of three people (John, Mary, and Sam) and asks you to find John's age. Since the question doesn't provide any of their actual ages, you need to solve for their ages by translating the relationships into algebraic expressions. If you let J = John, M = Mary, and S = Sam, you can express that John is 4 times older than Mary by writing $J = 4M$ and that Mary is 3 years younger than Sam by writing $M = S - 3$. Finally, you can write $S - 3 = 2(M - 3)$ to indicate that three years ago Sam was twice as old as Mary. Since you are looking for John's age, and since John's age is given only by $J = 4M$, you first need to find Mary's age. Each of the two other equations uses the unknowns M and S. Since you need Mary's age, you can solve for Sam's age in both of the equations, and then set the equations equal to each other.

$$
\begin{aligned}
M &= S - 3 \\
M + 3 &= S
\end{aligned}
$$

Also:

$$
\begin{aligned}
2(M - 3) &= S - 3 \\
2M - 6 &= S - 3 \\
2M - 3 &= S
\end{aligned}
$$

You now have two expressions equal to Sam's age. Setting these two expressions equal to each other gives you Mary's age:

$$
\begin{aligned}
2M - 3 &= M + 3 \\
M &= 6
\end{aligned}
$$

Now that you know Mary's age, you can figure out John's:

$$
\begin{aligned}
J &= 4M \\
&= 4 \cdot 6 \\
&= 24
\end{aligned}
$$

13. **(B)** *Fundamentals: Exponents*

This question tests your knowledge of the exponential law $x^a \cdot y^a = (xy)^a$:

$$24^{\frac{j}{3}} = 2^5 \cdot 3^5 \cdot 4^5$$

$$24^{\frac{j}{3}} = (2 \cdot 3 \cdot 4)^5$$

$$24^{\frac{j}{3}} = (24)^5$$

Since the bases are the same, you can set the exponents equal to each other:

$$\frac{j}{3} = 5$$

$$j = 15$$

14. **(B)** *Algebra: Polynomials*

In order to solve for k, you must use the information given about the division of $p(x)$. The polynomial version of long division states that any polynomial $p(x)$ can be written as $p(x) = (x-a) \cdot q(x) + R$, where $p(x)$ is the original polynomial, $(x-a)$ is the divisor, $q(x)$ is the quotient, and R is the remainder. You need to figure out how to use the information given about the remainder and the divisor to solve for k. The easiest way to solve for the unknown k is to have an expression with no other unknowns. In $p(x)$, you have the additional unknown x, but you can set x equal to anything you want. Try setting it equal to 2, which is a in the divisor $x - 2$. When you plug a into $p(x)$, you get $p(a) = (0) \cdot (q(a) + R)$, or $p(a) = R$. To find k, plug 2 into $p(x)$ and set the function equal to the remainder, 24.

$$24 = f(2)$$
$$24 = 2^3 + 2 \cdot 2^2 + 2k + 4$$
$$24 = 20 + 2k$$
$$4 = 2k$$
$$2 = k$$

15. **(C)** *Functions: Evaluating Functions*

This kind of operation/definition problem is a staple of the Math IC. Although the operation may seem intimidatingly unfamiliar, the definition of the operation is usually quite simple. This question provides the general rule $x \lozenge y = x^y - y^x$, and asks you to figure out $2 \lozenge s = 0$.

$$2 \lozenge s = 0$$
$$2^s - s^2 = 0$$
$$2^s = s^2$$

Plug in the possible answers, and you'll see that only 2 and 4 work.

16. **(D)** *Fundamentals: Word Problems*

The question gives you the fractional amounts George spent on food and books; it also tells you the dollar amount that remained for George to spend on his jacket. In order to determine the dollar amount George spent on books, you first need to determine the total dollar amount George spent. Since the only dollar amount given is the amount of the jacket, you should set up a proportion using the cost of the jacket and the proportion of money spent on it.

If George spent $\frac{1}{6} + \frac{2}{5} = \frac{17}{30}$ of his money on food and books, then the fractional amount of money spent on the jacket must be $\frac{13}{30}$. You know that $\frac{13}{30}$ of the total money is equal to \$104. The total amount of money George spent can then be calculated as:

$$\frac{104}{total} = \frac{13}{30}$$

$$104 \cdot \frac{30}{13} = total$$

$$240 = total$$

Now multiply the total amount by the fraction spent on books in order to find the dollar amount spent on books: $\frac{1}{6} \cdot 240 = 40$ dollars.

17. **(A)** *Algebra: Equation Solving, Absolute Value*

This question is a straightforward check to see whether you understand how absolute value signs work.

$$\begin{aligned} ||-x| - |2x|| - ||x| - |4x|| &= |x - 2x| - |-3x| \\ &= |-x| - |-3x| \\ &= x - 3x \\ &= -2x \end{aligned}$$

18. **(D)** *Plane Geometry: Lines and Angles*

Since lines l and m are parallel and cut by the transversal lines s and t, you can use the properties of transversals to figure out the value of θ. In the figure below, you can see that since $l \parallel m$, and since s is a transversal line, $\angle x = 85°$ means that $\angle 1 = 85°$. Additionally, since $\angle 2$ is supplementary to $\angle y$, $\angle 2 = 60°$. Because these angles are contained within a triangle, you know $\angle 1 + \angle 2 + \angle \theta = 180°$ and can solve for θ.

$$\angle \theta = 180° - \angle 1 - \angle 2$$
$$= 180° - 85° - 60°$$
$$= 35°$$

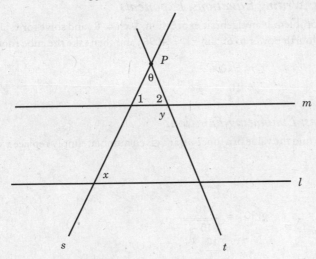

Note: Figure not drawn to scale.

19. **(E)** *Plane Geometry: Circles*

Whenever you see a quadrilateral inscribed within a circle such that one of the quadrilateral's vertices (or corners) is the center of the circle, then the following relationship must hold true true: $\angle BOC = 2\angle x$, as illustrated in the figure below.

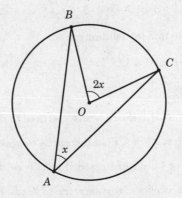

Since $\angle x = 20°$, $\angle BOC = 40°$. Now you can use the formula for the arc-length of a circle, $s = \dfrac{\theta}{360} \cdot 2\pi r$, where s is the arc-length, θ is $\angle BOC$, and r is the radius of the circle.

$$s = \frac{\theta}{180} \cdot \pi \cdot r$$
$$= \frac{40}{180} \cdot \pi \cdot 2.5$$
$$= 1.75$$

20. **(B)** *Algebra: Writing Equations, Exponents*

You should write this problem as an algebraic expression, $\sqrt[4]{x^3} = 8$, and solve for x. Use your calculator to raise both sides to the fourth power to obtain $x^3 = 4096$, and then take the cube root of both sides:

$$x = \sqrt[3]{4096}$$
$$= 16$$

21. **(C)** *Functions: Evaluating Functions*

When you are asked to find the value of a function at a given number, simply replace x with the number and solve the function.

$$g(x) = \frac{x}{\sqrt{x-1}}$$
$$g(10) = \frac{10}{\sqrt{10-1}}$$
$$= \frac{10}{3}$$

22. **(D)** *Algebra: Equation Solving*

When you see an inequality involving an absolute value expression, you can rewrite the inequality as two simpler inequalities. Because absolute value measures a number's distance from zero and ignores its sign, $7 - b$ can be a negative number smaller than –5 and have an absolute value greater than 5. You should rewrite the original inequality as:

$$7 - b > 5 \text{ or } 7 - b < -5$$

You can simplify these inequalities to find the solution set:

$$2 > b \text{ or } b > 12$$

23. **(C)** *Statistics: Probability*

When a probability question asks you for *at least* 3 heads, you need to remember that *at least* 3 means 3 or more—in this question, that translates to 3 or 4, since there are 4 tosses of the coin. You need to determine the number of sets in which either 3 or 4 heads are tossed; if you divide this number by the total number of possible sets, then you'll find the probability of tossing at least 3 heads. Remembering that the order of the tosses matters, you can find 5 possible sets that produce at least 3 heads: HHHT, HHTH, HTHH, THHH or HHHH, where H is a head and T is a tail. In order to find the total number, first determine the number of possible outcomes on each toss: 2, since you can toss either a head or a tail. If you have two possible outcomes on each of the four tosses, then the total number of sets is $2 \cdot 2 \cdot 2 \cdot 2 = 16$ sets. Of these 16 sets, 5 achieve at least 3 heads, so the probability of tossing at least 3 heads is $\frac{5}{16} = 0.3125$.

24. **(E)** *Miscellaneous Math: Complex Numbers*

You can solve this problem quickly if you recall that the values of i raised to an exponent recur in the following pattern:

$$i^1 = i \qquad\qquad i^5 = i \qquad\qquad i^9 = i$$

$$i^2 = -1 \qquad\qquad i^6 = -1 \qquad\qquad i^{10} = -1$$

$$i^3 = -i \qquad\qquad i^7 = -i \qquad\qquad \text{etc.}$$

$$i^4 = 1 \qquad\qquad i^8 = 1$$

If you know this pattern, you can quickly determine the values of each of the answer choices. For example, in choice (C), $i^{15} = -i$ and $i^{19} = -i$ because i raised to the exponents 15 and 19 has the same value as i raised to the exponent 3. The value of the expression in (C) is $i^{15} + i^{19} = -2i$, so you can rule (C) out. If you go through all the answer choices, you'll see that the only (E) is equal to zero.

There is a faster method of answering this question than the one mentioned above, but this method requires some deftness with exponential laws. The question asks for an expression that states $i^a + i^b = 0$. You can factor out i^a to rewrite the expression as $i^a(1 + i^{b-a}) = 0$, since the law of exponents says that $\frac{i^b}{i^a} = i^{b-a}$. If you divide both sides of $i^a(1 + i^{b-a}) = 0$ by i^a, you can then simplify the expression to $i^{b-a} = -1$. In order for this expression to be true, the exponent $b - a$ must be a multiple of 2 (since $i^2 = -1$), but not a multiple of 4 (since $i^4 = 1$). If you plug in values for b and a from the answer choices, you'll see that only the exponents from choice (E) fit these requirements when plugged into $b - a$: $31 - 25 = 6$.

25. **(C)** *Fundamentals: Exponents*

If you're familiar with the powers of 2, you can answer this question quickly without using a calculator. Rewriting the answer choices as powers of 2 allows you to compare their relative sizes based on the exponents.

$$2^{201} = 2^{201}$$
$$4^{100} = (2^2)^{100}$$
$$= 2^{200}$$
$$8^{70} = (2^3)^{70}$$
$$= 2^{210}$$
$$16^{50} = (2^4)^{50}$$
$$= 2^{200}$$
$$32^{39} = (2^5)^{39}$$
$$= 2^{195}$$

210 is the largest exponent, so (C) has the greatest value of the answer choices.

26. **(A)** *Plane Geometry: Triangles*

Since the triangle in this question is a right triangle, you know that $\theta_1 + \theta_2 = 90°$. Substituting $\frac{\theta_2}{2}$ for θ_1, you see that $\frac{3}{2}\theta_2 = 90°$ or $\theta_2 = 60°$. Now solve for a:

$$\tan\theta_2 = \frac{a}{7}$$
$$\tan 60° = \frac{a}{7}$$
$$7 \cdot \tan 60° = a$$
$$12.12 = a$$

You can also solve for a by using the properties of a 30-60-90 triangle. In 30-60-90 triangles, if the side opposite the 30° angle is x, then the side opposite the 60° angle is $x\sqrt{3}$.

27. **(D)** *Coordinate Geometry: Circles*

The equation for a circle of radius r centered at the point (h, k) is given by $(x - h)^2 + (y - k)^2 = r^2$. Since the circle in this problem is centered at the origin, its equation is $x^2 + y^2 = r^2$. To find r^2, plug the given (x, y) coordinates into the circle's equation.

$$1^2 + 6^2 = r^2$$
$$1 + 36 = r^2$$
$$37 = r^2$$

Replace r^2 with this value to get $x^2 + y^2 = 37$.

28. **(B)** *Fundamentals: Integers*

The basic calculus of even and odd numbers is summarized in the charts below.

×	Even	Odd
Even	Even	Even
Odd	Even	Odd

+	Even	Odd
Even	Even	Odd
Odd	Odd	Even

Although $m + n$ is even, the result when it is divided by 2 can be either even or odd ($6 \div 2 = 3$, for example), so option I cannot be right, and you can rule out answers (A) and (D). An odd number raised to any positive integer power remains odd, so m^n must be odd and $m^n + 1$ must be even; you can eliminate (E) since it states that none of the options must be even. Finally, $m^2 + n^2 + 1$ is an odd + odd + odd, which is always odd. Only option II is an even number, and (B) is correct.

29. **(A)** *Trigonometry: Pythagorean Identities*

You need to know the trigonometric identity $\cos^2\theta + \sin^2\theta = 1$ in order to answer this question.

$$
\begin{aligned}
(1 + \cos\theta)^2 - 2\cos\theta + \sin^2\theta &= 1 + 2\cos\theta + \cos^2\theta - 2\cos\theta + \sin^2\theta \\
&= 1 + \cos^2\theta + \sin^2\theta \\
&= 1 + 1 \\
&= 2
\end{aligned}
$$

30. **(D)** *Statistics: Arithmetic Mean*

A good approach to this problem is to represent the heights of the 5 people as a, b, c, d, and e, ordered from shortest to tallest. The median of a set is always the exact middle, so you can determine that c must be 68 inches tall. You know that two other people have the median height, so you can represent the possible heights in one of three ways: $(68, 68, 68, d, e)$, $(a, 68, 68, 68, e)$, and $(a, b, 68, 68, 68)$. Since the arithmetic mean is 70 inches, we know that the sum of all 5 of the heights is 350 inches. The sum of the two unknown heights must be $350 - 204 = 146$ inches. You can see that (A), which states that the tallest person is 70 inches, must be false because $146 - 70 = 76$ (it wouldn't make sense if the shortest person were 6 inches taller than the tallest person). Of the remaining answer choices, only (D) *must* be true, whereas the others may or may not be true. (D) must be true because the average of the two unknown heights is 73 inches ($146/2 = 73$), indicating either that both people are 73 inches tall or that one of them is taller than 73 inches.

31. **(E)** *Coordinate Geometry: Lines and Distance*

Remember that in an equation $y = mx + b$, the slope is equal to the coefficient m. In order to determine the slope of $y = h\left(\frac{x}{2} + 2\right)$, turn the expression into $y = mx + b$ form by plugging $\left(\frac{x}{2} + 2\right)$ into $h(x) = 3 - 4x$.

$$
\begin{aligned}
h\left(\frac{x}{2} + 2\right) &= 3 - 4\left(\frac{x}{2} + 2\right) \\
&= 3 - 2x - 8 \\
&= -2x - 5
\end{aligned}
$$

The slope of $y = -2x - 5$ is 2.

32. **(C)** *Solid Geometry: Prisms*

You need to visualize the cylinder in order to solve this problem. The figures below reveal how you obtain a point, a line, a rectangle, and an ellipse by intersecting a plane and a cylinder.

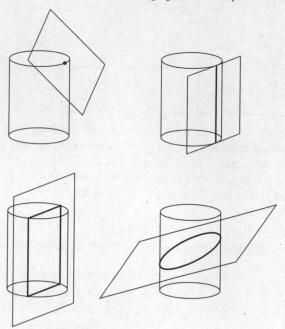

A triangle is not a possible result of this intersection.

33. **(A)** *Solid Geometry: Prisms*

The formulas for the surface area and volume of a cube with side length x are respectively $SA = 6x^2$ and $V = x^3$. Since the question states that the cube's surface area is equal to its volume, you should set these two formulas equal to each other and solve for x.

$$6x^2 = x^3$$
$$6 = x$$

34. **(D)** *Algebra: Polynomials*

If you haven't memorized the identities involving the sum and product of the roots of a quadratic equation, don't panic—you can figure them out using the quadratic formula. A quadratic equation of the form $ax^2 + bx + c = 0$ has roots $r_1, r_2 = \dfrac{-b \pm \sqrt{b^2 - 4ac}}{2a}$. If you add the roots together, $\sqrt{b^2 - 4ac}$ cancels out, and you are left with $r_1 + r_2 = -\dfrac{2b}{2a} = -\dfrac{b}{a}$. If you multiply the roots by each other, you get $r_1 \cdot r_2 = \dfrac{b^2 - b^2 + 4ac}{4a^2} = \dfrac{c}{a}$. The question states that the sum of the roots is 6, or $-\dfrac{b}{a} = 6$, and that the product of the roots is 7, or $\dfrac{c}{a} = 7$. Go through the answer choices and plug their coefficients into these identities; you'll find that only the coefficients of $2x^2 - 12x + 14 = 0$ work.

35. **(B)** *Plane Geometry: Lines and Angles, Triangles*

If a line parallel to the base of a triangle cuts through the triangle as shown in the figure below, then the following ratios of the sides must hold: $\frac{CB}{CE} = \frac{x+y}{x}$

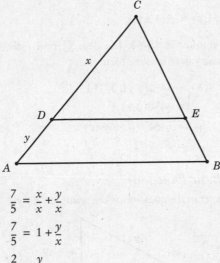

$$\frac{7}{5} = \frac{x}{x} + \frac{y}{x}$$

$$\frac{7}{5} = 1 + \frac{y}{x}$$

$$\frac{2}{5} = \frac{y}{x}$$

$$\frac{x}{y} = \frac{5}{2}, \text{ or } 2.5.$$

36. **(A)** *Functions: Transformations and Symmetry*

Since you are interested only in the point $Q(-1, 3)$, you can ignore the rest of the triangle. If a point (a, b) is reflected across the x-axis, it becomes $(a, -b)$. If a point (a, b) is reflected across the y-axis it becomes $(-a, b)$. When you reflect point $Q(-1, 3)$ across the x-axis, then your new point is $Q(-1, -3)$. When you reflect this new point across the y-axis, it will become $Q(1, -3)$.

37. **(B)** *Statistics: Permutations and Combinations*

The mathematical approach to this question is to consider 4-digit numbers as ordered sets of 4 individual numbers. Once you've seen the question in this light, you can find the answer by determining how many sets of numbers fulfill the conditions stated in the question. The first digit of the set can be a 1, 2, or a 3. The second digit of the set can be anything from 0 to 9—a total of 10 possibile numbers. The third digit can also be anything from 0 to 9, but the last number can be only a 1, 3, 5, 7, or 9—a total of 5 possibilities—since the question asks for odd 4-digit numbers. In order to determine how many sets satisfy the question's conditions, multiply $3 \cdot 10 \cdot 10 \cdot 5 = 1500$.

The intuitive approach to this question is to see that there are 3000 numbers from 1000 to 3999, inclusive. Of these 3000 numbers, half must be odd and half even; $3000/2 = 1500$ odd numbers. This approach can lead to trouble if you subtract 1000 from 3999 and then divide by 2; the result of your calculation would be 1449.5 odd numbers, and you might be tempted to choose (C)—or you might think the test writers screwed up. Because the question asks you for an inclusive set of numbers, you must include both of the end numbers in your calculation.

38. **(E)** *Algebra: Equation Solving, Exponential Growth and Decay*

You definitely need to memorize the formulas for growth and decay. Given an original amount A, a percentage rate of growth or decay r (written as a decimal), and a length of time t, you should know the following function for the amount present after t amount of time:

$$A(t) = A(1 \pm r)^t$$

In this question, the original amount is \$5450, the depreciation rate -0.07, and the length of time $2010 - 2002 = 8$ years. Plug these values into the formula:

$$
\begin{aligned}
A(8) &= 5450(1 - 0.07)^8 \\
&= 5450(0.93)^8 \\
&= 5450 \cdot (0.559582) \\
&= 3049.72
\end{aligned}
$$

39. **(D)** *Trigonometry: Basic Functions*

You can illustrate the conditions set in the question as the triangle below.

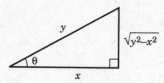

Since $\cos\theta = \dfrac{adjacent}{hypotenuse}$, you know that x is the side adjacent to the angle and that y is the hypotenuse of the triangle. You need the value of the side opposite the angle in order to find $\sin\theta$, and you can solve for the remaining side s using the Pythagorean Theorem.

$$
\begin{aligned}
x^2 + s^2 &= y^2 \\
s &= \pm\sqrt{y^2 - x^2}
\end{aligned}
$$

Since $\sin\theta = \dfrac{opposite}{hypotenuse}$, you can now write:

$$\sin\theta = \frac{\sqrt{y^2 - x^2}}{y}$$

40. **(D)** *Functions: Evaluating Functions*

Your first step should be to find the compound function $f(f(x))$. To do so, you need to plug $f(x) = ax + b$ into itself; in other words, plug $(ax + b)$ into $f(x) = ax + b$.

$$
\begin{aligned}
f(x) &= ax + b \\
f(f(x)) &= a \cdot f(x) + b \\
&= a(ax + b) + b \\
&= a^2 x + ab + b \\
&= a^2 x + b(a + 1)
\end{aligned}
$$

The question tells you that $f(f(x)) = x$, so you now have $x = a^2 x + b(a + 1)$. From this expression, you can discern that $a = \pm 1$, since x on the left-side of the equation has a coefficient of 1. You can also tell that $b(a + 1) = 0$, since there is no constant number on the left-side of the equation. In order for $b(a + 1) = 0$ to be true, either $a = -1$ or $b = 0$ if $a \neq -1$.

41. (E) *Solid Geometry: Prisms*

If the volume of the cube is 125, then the length of the cube's side must be $\sqrt[3]{125} = 5$ since $V_{cube} = s^3$.

From Figure 9, you can tell that the radius of the inscribed cone must be half the length of the cube's side, or $\frac{5}{2}$, and its height must be equal to the length of the cube's side, or 5.

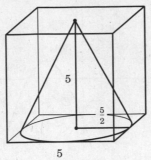

The volume of a circular cone is given by $V = \frac{1}{3}\pi r^2 h$. Plug the values you determined for the radius and height into this formula to obtain:

$$V = \frac{1}{3}\pi\left(\frac{5}{2}\right)^2 5$$

$$= 32.72$$

42. (E) *Plane Geometry: Polygons*

The area of a parallelogram with sides a and b and an included angle θ is given by the formula $A = a \cdot b \cdot \sin\theta$. You can plug in the values provided by the question to determine the length of the parallelogram's other side:

$$A = a \cdot 7 \cdot \sin 30°$$
$$42 = a \cdot 7 \cdot \frac{1}{2}$$
$$12 = a$$

You can now calculate the perimeter: $(2 \cdot 12) + (2 \cdot 7) = 38$.

43. (C) *Coordinate Geometry: Domain and Range*

Domain and range questions on the Math IC are often worded in tricky ways. The question provides you with a domain (a set of x values) for the function and asks you to find the range of values for $g(x)$. The simplest way to answer this question (and to avoid making errors) is to graph the given equation on your calculator, adjusting the graph window to the given domain (most graphing calculators will have a "Window" function where you can set the minimum and maximum x and y values to be displayed). For this function, set $x_{min} = 1$ and $x_{max} = 4$, then graph $g(x)$. Now you can find the range of the function by finding the maximum and minimum values for y shown on the screen; these values can be determined by your calculator. If your graph disappears off the top or the bottom of the screen, you will need to reset the window so you can see all values of y in the given domain. The graph of this function, shown below, is a downward opening parabola with vertex $= (2, 1)$.

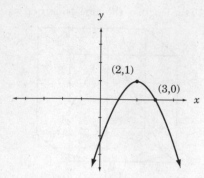

Over this particular domain, the largest value of y is 1 and the smallest value is –3, so the range of the function is $-3 \leq g(x) \leq 1$.

44. **(D)** *Miscellaneous Math: Sequences*

The question asks you for the nth term in the shown sequence, which is the same as asking for a general algebraic expression to represent the sequence. In the sequence given by the question, $n = 1$ indicates the first term of a sequence (in this case, 2), and $n = 2$ indicates the second (5).

The simplest way to find the correct algebraic expression for the sequence is to plug a value for n into each answer choice and then see which answer choice generates the number given in the sequence. Choose a value for n for which you know the outcome; for example, you know that when $n = 3$, you should end up with 10 when you plug 3 into the correct expression. Try to choose a value greater than $n = 2$. If you set n equal to 1 or 2 in this question, more than one expression will appear to work, and you'll eventually have to set $n = 3$. If you use $n = 3$, you'll see that only (D) generates 10.

45. **(C)** *Coordinate Geometry: Circles*

This question asks you to solve for b, which is the y-intercept of the line $y = x + b$. The question tells you that this line is tangent to a circle $x^2 + y^2 = 100$. The solution to this problem becomes apparent when you draw the circle and the line on a coordinate plane. Draw the circle, with its center at the origin and with a radius equal to 10 (since $100 = r^2$). The line can be tangent to the circle only at the two points shown in the figure below because the line's slope is equal to 1. A slope of 1 indicates that both the x and y values of the line increase as the graph moves to the right; furthermore, they increase at the same rate: when x gets bigger by one increment, so does y. The triangle formed by the line and the two axes in your drawing is a 45-45-90 triangle. If you draw the circle's radius at the point of tangency, you will divide the triangle into two smaller 45-45-90 triangles, with their hypotenuses along the axes. The two sides of the small triangle are equal to the length of the circle's radius. Since you know the radius of the circle is 10, you can use the Pythagorean Theorem to find b, where b represents the hypotenuse of the small triangle. $10^2 + 10^2 = b^2$; thus $b = \sqrt{200}$, or $b = \pm 10\sqrt{2}$.

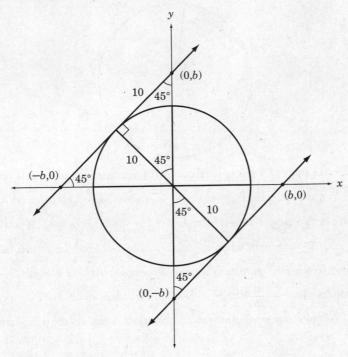

46. (D) *Functions: Transformations and Symmetry*

This question tests your knowledge of even and odd functions. An even function is defined as $f(x) = f(-x)$. It is a mathematical way of stating that the graph is symmetric across the y-axis. An odd function is defined as $f(-x) = -f(x)$; it is symmetric with respect to the origin. To determine whether the given functions are even, plug in $-x$ for x. If the value of the function remains the same, you've found an even function.

Option I is an even function because $|4 - (-x)^2| = |4 - x^2|$.

Option II is an odd function because $\dfrac{1}{x^3} \neq \dfrac{1}{(-x)^3} = -\dfrac{1}{x^3}$.

Option III is an even function because $\dfrac{1}{1 + x^2} = \dfrac{1}{1 + (-x)^2}$.

47. **(E)** *Plane Geometry: Circles*

The area of the shaded region is the difference between the area of the sector AOB and the area of the triangle $\triangle ABO$, as shown below.

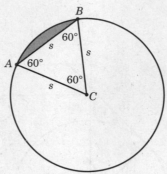

By drawing the radii AO and BO, you can see that $\triangle ABO$ is an equilateral triangle since each side has a length of 5. The fastest way to calculate the triangle's area is to use the formula $Area = \frac{\sqrt{3}}{4}s^2$, where s is the length of a side. You can also use the familiar formula $Area = \frac{1}{2} \cdot base \cdot height$. If you divide the triangle in half, you'll have a 30-60-90 triangle, where the adjacent side to the 60° angle has a length of $\frac{5}{2}$, and the hypotenuse has a length of 5. The opposite side to the 60° angle must have a length of $\frac{5\sqrt{3}}{2}$. The formula for the area of a sector is $Area = \frac{\theta}{360} \cdot \pi \cdot r^2$, where r is the radius and θ is the interior (or intercepted) angle. Since $\triangle ABO$ is equilateral, you know $\theta = 60°$. Subtract the area of the triangle from the area of the sector:

$$\left(\left(\frac{60}{360} \cdot \pi \cdot 5^2\right) - \left(\frac{\sqrt{3}}{4} \cdot 5^2\right)\right) = \left(\frac{25\pi}{6} - \frac{25\sqrt{3}}{4}\right)$$

The area of the shaded region is approximately 2.26.

48. **(B)** *Algebra: Equation Solving, Word Problems*

You should translate this word problem into an algebraic expression. If the original solution is 20% alcohol and totals 75ml, then there are $75 \cdot 0.2 = 15$ ml of alcohol in the original solution. If x is the amount of pure alcohol added to the solution, don't forget that adding x amount of alcohol increases the total volume by x as well. Since you want the end solution to be 40% (or 0.4) alcohol, you can write the expression as:

$$\frac{15 + x}{75 + x} = 0.4$$

$$15 + x = 0.4(75 + x)$$

$$15 + x = 30 + 0.4x$$

$$0.6x = 15$$

$$x = 25$$

49. **(C)** *Algebra: Polynomials*

Your first step should be to factor each function.

$$f(x) = x^2 - 12x + 35$$
$$= (x - 5)(x - 7)$$
$$g(x) = -x^2 + 4x + 21$$
$$= (7 - x)(3 + x)$$

Now divide $f(x)$ by $g(x)$ in their factored forms:

$$\frac{f(x)}{g(x)} = \frac{(x-5)(x-7)}{(7-x)(3+x)}$$

Notice that $(7 - x) = -(x - 7)$. If you cancel the terms, you get:

$$\frac{f(x)}{g(x)} = -\frac{x-5}{3+x}$$
$$= \frac{5-x}{3+x}$$

50. **(A)** *Miscellaneous Math: Logic*

Logic statements appear in the form of "If p, then q." The Math IC tests really only one rule of logic associated with such statements: when you have "If p, then q," its contrapositive, "If *not q*, then *not p*," is always true. You formulate the contrapositive of "If p, then q" by first switching p and q and then negating each of them (in other words, putting "not" in front of each): "if *not q*, then *not p*."

SAT II Math IC
Practice Test 2

MATH IC TEST 2 ANSWER SHEET

1. Ⓐ Ⓑ Ⓒ Ⓓ Ⓔ	18. Ⓐ Ⓑ Ⓒ Ⓓ Ⓔ	35. Ⓐ Ⓑ Ⓒ Ⓓ Ⓔ
2. Ⓐ Ⓑ Ⓒ Ⓓ Ⓔ	19. Ⓐ Ⓑ Ⓒ Ⓓ Ⓔ	36. Ⓐ Ⓑ Ⓒ Ⓓ Ⓔ
3. Ⓐ Ⓑ Ⓒ Ⓓ Ⓔ	20. Ⓐ Ⓑ Ⓒ Ⓓ Ⓔ	37. Ⓐ Ⓑ Ⓒ Ⓓ Ⓔ
4. Ⓐ Ⓑ Ⓒ Ⓓ Ⓔ	21. Ⓐ Ⓑ Ⓒ Ⓓ Ⓔ	38. Ⓐ Ⓑ Ⓒ Ⓓ Ⓔ
5. Ⓐ Ⓑ Ⓒ Ⓓ Ⓔ	22. Ⓐ Ⓑ Ⓒ Ⓓ Ⓔ	39. Ⓐ Ⓑ Ⓒ Ⓓ Ⓔ
6. Ⓐ Ⓑ Ⓒ Ⓓ Ⓔ	23. Ⓐ Ⓑ Ⓒ Ⓓ Ⓔ	40. Ⓐ Ⓑ Ⓒ Ⓓ Ⓔ
7. Ⓐ Ⓑ Ⓒ Ⓓ Ⓔ	24. Ⓐ Ⓑ Ⓒ Ⓓ Ⓔ	41. Ⓐ Ⓑ Ⓒ Ⓓ Ⓔ
8. Ⓐ Ⓑ Ⓒ Ⓓ Ⓔ	25. Ⓐ Ⓑ Ⓒ Ⓓ Ⓔ	42. Ⓐ Ⓑ Ⓒ Ⓓ Ⓔ
9. Ⓐ Ⓑ Ⓒ Ⓓ Ⓔ	26. Ⓐ Ⓑ Ⓒ Ⓓ Ⓔ	43. Ⓐ Ⓑ Ⓒ Ⓓ Ⓔ
10. Ⓐ Ⓑ Ⓒ Ⓓ Ⓔ	27. Ⓐ Ⓑ Ⓒ Ⓓ Ⓔ	44. Ⓐ Ⓑ Ⓒ Ⓓ Ⓔ
11. Ⓐ Ⓑ Ⓒ Ⓓ Ⓔ	28. Ⓐ Ⓑ Ⓒ Ⓓ Ⓔ	45. Ⓐ Ⓑ Ⓒ Ⓓ Ⓔ
12. Ⓐ Ⓑ Ⓒ Ⓓ Ⓔ	29. Ⓐ Ⓑ Ⓒ Ⓓ Ⓔ	46. Ⓐ Ⓑ Ⓒ Ⓓ Ⓔ
13. Ⓐ Ⓑ Ⓒ Ⓓ Ⓔ	30. Ⓐ Ⓑ Ⓒ Ⓓ Ⓔ	47. Ⓐ Ⓑ Ⓒ Ⓓ Ⓔ
14. Ⓐ Ⓑ Ⓒ Ⓓ Ⓔ	31. Ⓐ Ⓑ Ⓒ Ⓓ Ⓔ	48. Ⓐ Ⓑ Ⓒ Ⓓ Ⓔ
15. Ⓐ Ⓑ Ⓒ Ⓓ Ⓔ	32. Ⓐ Ⓑ Ⓒ Ⓓ Ⓔ	49. Ⓐ Ⓑ Ⓒ Ⓓ Ⓔ
16. Ⓐ Ⓑ Ⓒ Ⓓ Ⓔ	33. Ⓐ Ⓑ Ⓒ Ⓓ Ⓔ	50. Ⓐ Ⓑ Ⓒ Ⓓ Ⓔ
17. Ⓐ Ⓑ Ⓒ Ⓓ Ⓔ	34. Ⓐ Ⓑ Ⓒ Ⓓ Ⓔ	

REFERENCE INFORMATION

THE FOLLOWING INFORMATION IS FOR YOUR REFERENCE IN ANSWERING SOME OF THE QUESTIONS IN THIS TEST:

Volume of a right circular cone with radius r and height h: $V = \frac{1}{3}\pi r^2 h$

Lateral area of a right circular cone with circumference of the base c and slaight height ℓ: $S = \frac{1}{2}c\ell$

Volume of a sphere with radius r: $V = \frac{4}{3}\pi r^3$

Surface area of a sphere with radius r: $S = 4\pi r^2$

Volume of a pyramid with base area B and height h: $V = \frac{1}{3}Bh$

MATHEMATICS LEVEL IC TEST

For each of the following problems, decide which is the BEST of the choices given. If the exact numerical value is not one of the choices, select the choice that best approximates this value. Then fill in the corresponding oval on the answer sheet.

<u>Notes:</u> (1) A calculator will be necessary for answering some (but not all) of the questions in this test. For each question you will have to decide whether or not you should use a calcuator. The calculator you use must be at least a scientific calculator; programmable calculators and calculators that can display graphs are permitted.

(2) For some questions in this test you may need to decide whether your calculator should be in radian or degree mode.

(3) Figures that accompany problems in this test are intended to provide information useful in solving the problems. They are drawn as accurately as possible EXCEPT when it is stated in a specific problem that its figure is not drawn to scale. All figures lie in a plane unless otherwise indicated.

(4) Unless otherwise specified, the domain of any function f is assumed to be the set of all real numbers x for which $f(x)$ is a real number.

(5) Reference information that may be useful in answering the questions in this test can be found on the page preceding Question 1.

USE THIS SPACE FOR SCRATCHWORK.

1. If $a + b + 5 = 9$, then $3a + 3b =$

    (A) 14
    (B) 12
    (C) 10
    (D) 8
    (E) 6

2. If $f(x) = 16x^2 + 4x - 2$, then $f\left(\frac{3}{4}\right) =$

    (A) 9.75
    (B) 10
    (C) 10.25
    (D) 11
    (E) 11.75

3. Which of the following integers has the <u>smallest</u> remainder when it is divided by 13 ?

    (A) 199
    (B) 198
    (C) 197
    (D) 196
    (E) 195

GO ON TO THE NEXT PAGE

4. If John can answer a question every 12 seconds, then how many questions could he answer in one hour?

    (A) 300
    (B) 360
    (C) 400
    (D) 480
    (E) 500

5. If $3 \cdot 5^{x+2} = 375$, then $x =$

    (A) -3
    (B) -1
    (C) 1
    (D) 2
    (E) 3

6. What is the distance between the points $(1, 4)$ and $(4, 1)$?

    (A) 0
    (B) 3
    (C) 4.24
    (D) 4.84
    (E) 5.24

7. $2x^2 - 12x + 10 =$

    (A) $(x-1)(2x+10)$
    (B) $(2x-1)(x+5)$
    (C) $(2x-1)(x-5)$
    (D) $2(x-1)(x-5)$
    (E) $2(x+1)(x-5)$

8. If $x < 0$ and $x^4 = 81$, then $x^3 =$

    (A) -27
    (B) -9
    (C) 0
    (D) 9
    (E) 27

GO ON TO THE NEXT PAGE

USE THIS SPACE FOR SCRATCHWORK.

9. If $g(x) = |1 - x|$ and $h(x) = \frac{1}{x}$, then $g\left(h\left(-\frac{1}{3}\right)\right) =$

   (A) −4

   (B) −2

   (C) $\frac{4}{3}$

   (D) 2

   (E) 4

10. If $a = 5$, then $\dfrac{2a^{200}}{7a^{198}} =$

   (A) 7

   (B) 7.14

   (C) 8.25

   (D) 9.14

   (E) 25

11. If $x^3 + x^2 - 5x + 1 = 0$ and $x^3 + x^2 + 6x - 20 = 1$, then $x =$

   (A) −1.06

   (B) 0

   (C) 2

   (D) 2.25

   (E) 5.14

12. In Figure 1, $AD \parallel BC$. What is the value of θ?

   (A) $\frac{x}{2}$

   (B) $180 + x$

   (C) $180 - x$

   (D) $180 + 2x$

   (E) $180 - 2x$

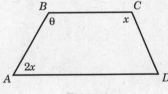

Figure 1

GO ON TO THE NEXT PAGE

13. Given positive integers m and n, then $m \cdot n - 1$ must be an even integer if:

   I. m is odd
   II. n is odd
   III. m or n is even

   (A) I only
   (B) II only
   (C) III only
   (D) I and II only
   (E) None of the above

14. If $(2x + 2y)^2 = 16$ and $x^2 + y^2 = 2$, then $xy =$

   (A) 0
   (B) $\frac{1}{2}$
   (C) 1
   (D) $\frac{3}{2}$
   (E) 8

15. In Figure 2, if $a = 5$ and $b = 6$, then which of the following could <u>not</u> be the value of c?

   (A) 1.01
   (B) 9.01
   (C) 10.01
   (D) 10.99
   (E) 11.01

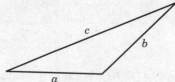

Note: Figure not drawn to scale.
Figure 2

16. The fifth root of the cube of a number is 27. Which of the following is the number?

   (A) 244
   (B) 243
   (C) 27
   (D) 7.22
   (E) 3

GO ON TO THE NEXT PAGE

17. The line $3x + 4y = 7$ is perpendicular to which of the following lines?

    (A) $4x - 3y = 5$
    (B) $4x + 3y = 5$
    (C) $3x - 4y = 7$
    (D) $3x - 4y = 5$
    (E) $3x + 4y = 5$

18. If $g(x) = x^3$, then the value of $g(1) - g(-3) =$

    (A) 28
    (B) 4
    (C) −4
    (D) −26
    (E) −28

19. What is the remainder when $x^5 + 3x^3 + 2x - 3$ is divided by $x + 1$?

    (A) 9
    (B) 6
    (C) −3
    (D) −9
    (E) −10

20. If $i^2 = -1$, then $i^3 + i^2 + i + 1 =$

    (A) $-2i$
    (B) $-i$
    (C) 0
    (D) 1
    (E) $2i$

21. Which of the following is the solution set to the inequality $(x - 3)(x - 2) < 0$?

    (A) $2 \le x \le 3$
    (B) $2 < x < 3$
    (C) $2 < x$
    (D) $3 < x$
    (E) All real values of x

GO ON TO THE NEXT PAGE

22. In Figure 3, the arithmetic mean (average) of angles 1, 2, 3, and 4 is 120°. What is the value of ∠5?

    (A) 60°
    (B) 80°
    (C) 118°
    (D) 120°
    (E) 122°

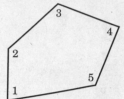

Note: Figure not drawn to scale.

Figure 3

23. When the square of a number n is added to the number n, the resulting value is 2. Which of the following could be the number n?

    (A) −4
    (B) −2
    (C) −1
    (D) 0.5
    (E) 2

24. If $x^2 = y^2$, which of the following must be true?

    (A) x and y are both positive numbers
    (B) x and y are both negative numbers
    (C) $x = y$
    (D) $x = -y$
    (E) $x = y$ or $x = -y$

25. If $0 \le \theta < 90°$, and $\sin^2\theta = \tan\theta - \cos^2\theta$, then $\tan\theta =$

    (A) −2
    (B) −1.5
    (C) −1
    (D) 0
    (E) 1

26. The sum of the perimeter and area of a square is 100. What is the length of one of its sides?

    (A) 1.2
    (B) 4.1
    (C) 8.2
    (D) 10
    (E) 12.2

GO ON TO THE NEXT PAGE

USE THIS SPACE FOR SCRATCHWORK.

27. If $h(x) = 4x + 1$ and $h(f(7)) = 13$, then $f(7) =$

 (A) 3
 (B) 4.6
 (C) 7
 (D) 9
 (E) Not enough information to tell

28. If $x - y = 8$ and $x^2 - y^2 = 56$, then $\frac{x}{y} =$

 (A) 37.5
 (B) 15
 (C) −3.75
 (D) −15
 (E) −25

29. In Figure 4, what is the value of x ?

 (A) 30°
 (B) 60°
 (C) 61°
 (D) 90°
 (E) 91°

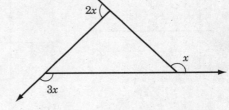

Note: Figure not drawn to scale.

Figure 4

30. If the origin is the midpoint of the line segment between the points $(-1, 4)$ and (x, y), then $(x, y) =$

 (A) $(-4, 1)$
 (B) $(-4, -1)$
 (C) $(1, 4)$
 (D) $(1, -4)$
 (E) $(-1, -4)$

31. The average (arithmetic mean) height of 3 people is 70 inches. The average height of 5 other people is 66 inches. What is the average height of all 8 people?

 (A) 69.66 inches
 (B) 69.5 inches
 (C) 69 inches
 (D) 68 inches
 (E) 67.5 inches

GO ON TO THE NEXT PAGE

32. If the range of the function $f(x) = \dfrac{2x+5}{3}$ is given by $2 \le f(x) \le 3$, then what is the domain of the function?

    (A) $\dfrac{-1}{2} < x < \dfrac{1}{2}$

    (B) $\dfrac{1}{2} < x < 2$

    (C) $\dfrac{1}{2} \le x \le 2$

    (D) $2 \le x \le \dfrac{11}{3}$

    (E) $2 \le x \le 4$

33. If $f(x) = \sqrt{x}$ and $h(x) = x - 4$, then which of the following could be a portion of the graph of $f(h(x))$?

    (A)
    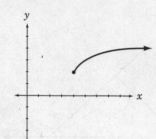

    (B)
    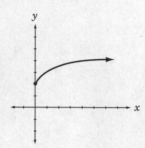

    (C)
    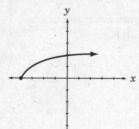

    (D)
    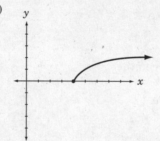

    (E)
    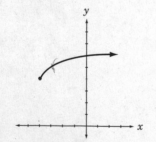

GO ON TO THE NEXT PAGE

USE THIS SPACE FOR SCRATCHWORK.

34. If a quadrilateral with vertices $(-1, -1)$, $(2, 3)$, $(4, -1)$, and (j, k) is a rhombus, then $(j, k) =$

   (A) $(4, 3)$
   (B) $(6, 2)$
   (C) $(6, 3)$
   (D) $(7, 3)$
   (E) $(7, 4)$

35. A function $f(x)$ has the property that $f(-x) = -f(x)$ for all real values of x. If the point $(2, 65)$ is on the graph of $y = f(x)$, then which of the following points <u>must</u> also be on the graph?

   (A) $(65, 2)$
   (B) $(65, -2)$
   (C) $(0, 65)$
   (D) $(-2, 65)$
   (E) $(-2, -65)$

36. What is the maximum value of the function $f(x) = 3 + 4x - x^2$ on the interval $0 \le x \le 5$?

   (A) 2
   (B) 7
   (C) 0
   (D) -7.5
   (E) It has no maximum value over the specified interval.

37. A right circular cylinder has a height h, which is equal to twice the cylinder's diameter. In terms of h, what is the volume of the cylinder?

   (A) $\dfrac{\pi}{16}h^2$

   (B) $\dfrac{\pi}{16}h^3$

   (C) $\dfrac{\pi}{4}h^3$

   (D) $\dfrac{\pi}{2}h^3$

   (E) πh^3

GO ON TO THE NEXT PAGE

38. If $p(x) = 2 - x - x^2$ and $q(x) = x^2 - 3x + 2$, then for all x such that $x \neq -2$ and $x \neq 1$, $\dfrac{q(x)}{p(x)} =$

    (A) $\dfrac{x-2}{2+x}$

    (B) 1

    (C) $\dfrac{2-x}{2+x}$

    (D) $\dfrac{2-x}{x-2}$

    (E) $x + 2$

39. John is standing 100 feet away from the base of a water tower. He measures the angle from the ground to his line of sight of the top of the tower to be $42°$. How many feet tall is the tower?

    (A) 90.04
    (B) 92.18
    (C) 96.52
    (D) 100.11
    (E) 111.06

40. If the triangle in Figure 5 is rotated about side BC, then what is the volume of the resulting cone?

    (A) $4\sqrt{7}\pi$
    (B) $\sqrt{7}\pi$
    (C) 7π
    (D) 8π
    (E) $8\sqrt{2}\pi$

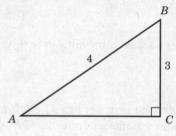

Note: Figure not drawn to scale.

Figure 5

41. An equilateral triangle and a square have equal perimeters. What is the ratio of the area of the triangle to the area of the square?

    (A) $\dfrac{\sqrt{3}}{16}$

    (B) $\dfrac{\sqrt{3}}{9}$

    (C) $\dfrac{2}{9}\sqrt{3}$

    (D) $\dfrac{4}{9}\sqrt{3}$

    (E) $\sqrt{3}$

GO ON TO THE NEXT PAGE

42. If $f(x) = 2x - 5$ and $g(f(x)) = x$, then $g(7) =$

(A) −7
(B) −1
(C) 2
(D) 3
(E) 6

43. A positive integer n is divided by 11. What is the probability that the remainder will be an even integer?

(A) $\frac{5}{11}$

(B) $\frac{6}{11}$

(C) $\frac{7}{11}$

(D) $\frac{1}{2}$

(E) 1

44. The acceleration of an object falling through the air with resistance is directly proportional to the square of its velocity. If the acceleration of an object is 10 meters per second squared (m/s^2) when its velocity is 125 m/s^2, what is its acceleration (in m/s^2) when the velocity is 150 m/s^2 ?

(A) 14.4
(B) 14
(C) 12.6
(D) 10.1
(E) 9

45. If a cube has a long diagonal of length d, which of the following represents the volume of the cube in terms of d?

(A) $\frac{d^3}{3}$

(B) $\frac{d^3}{9}$

(C) $\frac{\sqrt{3}d^3}{9}$

(D) $\frac{\sqrt{3}d^3}{3}$

(E) Not enough information to tell

GO ON TO THE NEXT PAGE

46. The statement, "If the sun is shining, then the grass is dry" is logically equivalent to which of the following?

    (A) If the sun is not shining, then the grass is not dry.
    (B) If the grass is not dry, then the sun is shining.
    (C) If the sun is shining, then the grass is not dry.
    (D) If the grass is not dry, then the sun is not shining.
    (E) If the grass is dry, then the sun is shining.

47. $(\sin x + \cos x)^2 + (\sin x - \cos x)^2 =$

    (A) -2
    (B) $4 \sin x \cos x$
    (C) 0
    (D) 1
    (E) 2

48. In Figure 6, a square $ABCD$ is inscribed within circle O. If the area of the square is 8, which of the following is the approximate area of the shaded region?

    (A) 1.14
    (B) 1.64
    (C) 2.14
    (D) 2.64
    (E) 3.14

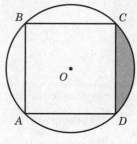

Figure 6

GO ON TO THE NEXT PAGE

USE THIS SPACE FOR SCRATCHWORK.

49. In Figure 7, if $(BD)^2 = 36$, then what is the value of $AD \cdot DC$?

   (A) 6
   (B) 24
   (C) 30
   (D) 36
   (E) Not enough information to tell

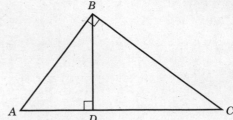

Figure 7

50. In Figure 8, what is the value (in degrees) of $x^2 + \dfrac{1}{x^2}$?

   (A) 8102
   (B) 8100
   (C) 8098
   (D) 8097
   (E) 8096

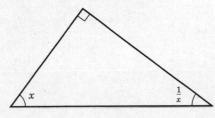

Figure 8

S T O P

IF YOU FINISH BEFORE TIME IS CALLED, YOU MAY CHECK YOUR WORK ON THIS TEST ONLY.
DO NOT TURN TO ANY OTHER TEST IN THIS BOOK.

SAT II Math IC
Practice Test 2
Explanations

Calculating Your Score

Question Number	Correct Answer	Right	Wrong	Question Number	Correct Answer	Right	Wrong	Question Number	Correct Answer	Right	Wrong
1.	B	—	—	18.	A	—	—	35.	E	—	—
2.	B	—	—	19.	D	—	—	36.	B	—	—
3.	E	—	—	20.	C	—	—	37.	B	—	—
4.	A	—	—	21.	B	—	—	38.	C	—	—
5.	C	—	—	22.	A	—	—	39.	A	—	—
6.	C	—	—	23.	B	—	—	40.	C	—	—
7.	D	—	—	24.	E	—	—	41.	D	—	—
8.	A	—	—	25.	E	—	—	42.	E	—	—
9.	E	—	—	26.	C	—	—	43.	B	—	—
10.	B	—	—	27.	A	—	—	44.	A	—	—
11.	C	—	—	28.	D	—	—	45.	C	—	—
12.	E	—	—	29.	B	—	—	46.	D	—	—
13.	D	—	—	30.	D	—	—	47.	E	—	—
14.	C	—	—	31.	E	—	—	48.	A	—	—
15.	E	—	—	32.	C	—	—	49.	D	—	—
16.	B	—	—	33.	D	—	—	50.	C	—	—
17.	A			34.	D						

Your raw score for the SAT II Math IC test is calculated from the number of questions you answer correctly and incorrectly. Once you have determined your composite score, use the conversion table on page 18 of this book to calculate your scaled score. To calculate your raw score, count the number of questions you answered correctly: _____
$$A$$

Count the number of questions you answered incorrectly, and multiply that number by $\frac{1}{4}$:

$$\underset{B}{\rule{3cm}{0.4pt}} \times \frac{1}{4} = \underset{C}{\rule{3cm}{0.4pt}}$$

Subtract the value in field C from value in field A: _____
$$D$$

Round the number in field D to the nearest whole number. This is your raw score: _____
$$E$$

Math IC Test 2 Explanations

1. **(B)** *Algebra: Equation Solving*

To find $3a + 3b$, first solve for $a + b$. Since $a + b + 5 = 9$, you can subtract 5 from each side to get $a + b = 4$. Now multiply both sides of this equation by 3 to find:

$$3(a + b) = 3 \cdot 4$$
$$3a + 3b = 12$$

2. **(B)** *Functions: Evaluating Functions*

In order to find $f\left(\frac{3}{4}\right)$, plug in $\frac{3}{4}$ for x in $f(x) = 16x^2 + 4x - 2$:

$$\begin{aligned}
f\left(\frac{3}{4}\right) &= 16 \cdot \left(\frac{3}{4}\right)^2 + 4 \cdot \left(\frac{3}{4}\right) - 2 \\
&= 16 \cdot \frac{9}{16} + 4 \cdot \frac{3}{4} - 2 \\
&= 9 + 3 - 2 \\
&= 10
\end{aligned}$$

3. **(E)** *Fundamentals: Integers*

When one integer does not divide evenly by another integer, it leaves behind a remainder. For example, 11 divided by 5 leaves behind a remainder of 1. For this problem, divide each of the answer choices by 13 and examine the remainder.

$$\begin{aligned}
199 &= 13 \cdot 15 + 4 \\
198 &= 13 \cdot 15 + 3 \\
197 &= 13 \cdot 15 + 2 \\
196 &= 13 \cdot 15 + 1 \\
195 &= 13 \cdot 15 + 0
\end{aligned}$$

0 is the smallest possible remainder, so (E) is correct.

4. **(A)** *Fundamentals: Word Problems*

This question tells you that John can answer one question every 12 seconds and asks you how many questions he can answer in one hour. Because an hour is a different unit of measurement from a second, you need to translate seconds into an hour:

$$\frac{1 \text{ question}}{12 \text{ seconds}} \times \frac{60 \text{ seconds}}{1 \text{ minute}} \times \frac{60 \text{ minutes}}{1 \text{ hour}} = \frac{300 \text{ questions}}{1 \text{ hour}}$$

The first term in this expression means "1 question per 12 seconds." The second and third terms are each equal to 1 (60 seconds is the same as one minute, and 60 minutes is the same as 1 hour). Multiplying by the second and third terms converts the expression to show how many questions John answers per hour, keeping the original proportion the same. The seconds and minutes cancel because they are found in both the numerator and denominator of the expression, leaving you with the number of questions per hour.

5. **(C)** *Algebra: Equation Solving, Logarithms*

To solve for x, first divide both sides of the equation by 3.

$$\frac{3 \cdot 5^{x+2}}{3} = \frac{375}{3}$$
$$5^{x+2} = 125$$

Since x is in the exponent, you need to rewrite the equation as a logarithm:

$$x + 2 = \log_5 125$$

$\log_5 125 = 3$ because $125 = 5^3$. So now you have:

$$x + 2 = 3$$
$$x = 1$$

You can answer this question without using logarithms if you recognize during the second step that $125 = 5^3$. In that case, you would have the equation:

$$5^{x+2} = 5^3$$

According to the law of exponents, since the bases are equal, the exponents must also be equal.

$$x + 2 = 3$$
$$x = 1$$

6. (C) *Coordinate Geometry: Lines and Distance*

This is a straightforward application of the distance formula, which you should definitely memorize for the Math IC. The formula for the distance between two points (x_1, y_1) and (x_2, y_2) in a plane is:

$$d = \sqrt{(x_1 - x_2)^2 + (y_1 - y_2)^2}$$

Plug the coordinates into this formula:

$$= \sqrt{(1 - 4)^2 + (4 - 1)^2}$$
$$= \sqrt{(-3)^2 + (3)^2}$$
$$= \sqrt{9 + 9}$$
$$= \sqrt{18}$$
$$= 4.24$$

7. (D) *Algebra: Polynomials*

This question asks you to factor the equation. Factoring an equation is always a little tricky, but you can simplify this equation by first factoring out the 2:

$$2x^2 - 12x + 10 = 2(x^2 - 6x + 5)$$
$$= 2(x - 1)(x - 5)$$

If you want to verify this answer, multiply it out to see whether you get the original equation.

8. (A) *Algebra: Equation Solving*

To find the value of x, take the fourth root of both sides of $x^4 = 81$. You need to remember that an even root (such as the square root, the fourth root, the sixth root, etc.) can be a positive or negative number. The fourth root of 81 is $x = \pm 3$. The question states that $x < 0$, which means that x is a negative number, so x must be -3 and $x^3 = -27$.

9. **(E)** *Functions: Compound Functions*

In order to solve the compound function $g\left(h\left(-\frac{1}{3}\right)\right)$, you should first find $h\left(-\frac{1}{3}\right)$. Substitute $-\frac{1}{3}$ for x in $h(x) = \frac{1}{x}$:

$$h\left(-\frac{1}{3}\right) = \frac{1}{-\frac{1}{3}}$$
$$= -3$$

Now, plug this value into $g(x)$.

$$g(-3) = |1 - (-3)|$$
$$= |1 + 3|$$
$$= 4$$

10. **(B)** *Fundamentals: Exponents*

Before you plug in $a = 5$, you should simplify the expression using the law of exponents. If you don't simplify the expression, your calculator will probably choke on the large numbers.

$$\frac{2a^{200}}{7a^{198}} = \frac{2}{7}a^{200-198}$$
$$= \frac{2}{7}a^{2}$$

Now you can plug in $a = 5$.

$$= \frac{2}{7}5^{2}$$
$$= \frac{2}{7} \cdot 25$$
$$= \frac{50}{7}$$
$$= 7.14$$

11. **(C)** *Algebra: Equation Solving*

You need to solve for x given these two equations: $x^3 + x^2 - 5x + 1 = 0$ and $x^3 + x^2 + 6x - 20 = 1$. Usually when you have two equations with the same unknown variable, you can set the equations equal to each other to find the unknown. In this case, you first need to make the two equations equal in value. To do this, subtract 1 from both sides of the second equation, turning it into $x^3 + x^2 + 6x - 21 = 0$. Now that both equations are equal to 0, you can set them equal to each other and solve for x:

$$x^3 + x^2 - 5x + 1 = x^3 + x^2 + 6x - 21$$
$$-5x + 1 = 6x - 21$$
$$22 = 11x$$
$$2 = x$$

12. (E) *Plane Geometry: Lines and Angles*

If you imagine AD and BC extending beyond the polygon, you can see that they are parallel lines cut by the transversal AB. Knowing this about the lines will allow you to solve for θ using the properties of parallel lines cut by a transversal.

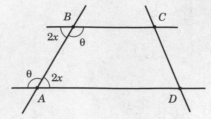

As you can see from the figure, $\angle ABC$ and $\angle DAB$ are supplementary. $\angle BCD$ is merely a red herring. Now you know:

$$\angle ABC + \angle DAB = 180°$$
$$\theta + 2x = 180°$$
$$\theta = 180 - 2x$$

13. (D) *Fundamentals: Integers*

$(x-1)$ can be an even integer only if x is odd. Now suppose, as the question states, that $x = mn$. A product of two integers can be odd only if both of the integers are odd, according to the basic rules of operations on odd and even numbers. Both options I and II, which state respectively that m and n are odd, must be true then, and (D) is the correct answer.

14. (C) *Algebra: Equation Solving*

Your first instinct should be to multiply out $(2x + 2y)^2$. Often, when the Math IC writers give you equations in a factored form, multiplying the equations out will help you spot the solution. The opposite also applies: when you're presented with an unfactored equation, you should attempt to factor it.

$$(2x + 2y)^2 = 4x^2 + 8xy + 4y^2$$

Set this new expression equal to 16, and factor out the 4:

$$4x^2 + 8xy + 4y^2 = 16$$
$$x^2 + 2xy + y^2 = 4$$

Now you need to recognize that you can substitute 2 for $x^2 + y^2$:

$$2xy + 2 = 4$$
$$2xy = 2$$
$$xy = 1$$

15. (E) *Plane Geometry: Triangles*

This question tests your understanding of the triangle inequality rule. The triangle inequality rule states that in order for a triangle with sides a, b, and c to be an actual triangle, the following relation among the sides must hold: $|a - b| < c < a + b$. If you apply this rule to the question, you get:

$$|5 - 6| < c < 5 + 6$$
$$1 < c < 11$$

Only answer choice (E) falls outside of this range, so it is the correct answer.

16. (B) *Algebra: Writing Equations*

Your first step should be to translate "the fifth root of the cube of a number is 27" into an algebraic expression, in which x represents the unknown number. Then you can solve for x.

$$\sqrt[5]{x^3} = 27$$

You can rewrite the left side of the expression as x raised to a fractional exponent:

$$x^{3/5} = 27$$

Now raise both sides of the expression to the $\frac{5}{3}$ power to solve for x:

$$(x^{3/5})^{5/3} = 27^{5/3}$$
$$x = 27^{5/3}$$
$$x = 243$$

17. (A) *Coordinate Geometry: Lines and Distance*

If a line is given in the standard form $Ax + By = C$, then the slope of the line is $m = -\frac{A}{B}$. A perpendicular line has the slope $m_\perp = -\frac{1}{m}$. The equation given in the question, $3x + 4y = 7$, has a slope of $m = -\frac{3}{4}$; therefore, a perpendicular line must have a slope $m_\perp = \frac{4}{3}$. If $\frac{4}{3} = -\frac{A}{B}$, then the equation of the line must include $4x - 3y$ or $-4x + 3y$; thus choice (A) is correct.

18. (A) *Functions: Evaluating Functions*

If $g(x) = x^3$, then $g(1) = 1^3 = 1$ and $g(-3) = (-3)^3 = -27$.

$$g(1) - g(-3) = 1 - (-27)$$
$$= 1 + 27$$
$$= 28$$

19. (D) *Algebra: Polynomials*

You need to know the polynomial version of long division, which states that any polynomial $p(x)$ can be written as $p(x) = (x - a) \cdot q(x) + R$, where $p(x)$ is the original polynomial, $(x - a)$ is the divisor, $q(x)$ is the quotient, and R is the remainder. The most efficient way to find the remainder is to plug a into $p(x)$, since $p(a) = (0) \cdot q(a) + R$, or $p(a) = R$. The divisor in this question is $x + 1$; thus $a = -1$:

$$p(x) = x^5 + 3x^3 + 2x - 3$$
$$p(-1) = (-1)^5 + 3(-1)^3 + 2(-1) - 3$$
$$= -1 - 3 - 2 - 3$$
$$= -9$$

20. (C) *Miscellaneous Math: Complex Numbers*

Problems involving complex numbers will probably appear once or twice on the Math IC, but you'll always be given the definition $i^2 = -1$. If n is a positive integer, then i^n can take on 4 possible values: $i^1 = i$, $i^2 = -1$, $i^3 = -i$, $i^4 = 1$, $i^5 = i$, $i^6 = -1$, etc. Calculate the value of each term in this expression to find the answer:

$$i^3 + i^2 + i + 1 = -i - 1 + i + 1$$
$$= 0$$

21. (B) *Algebra: Equation Solving, Inequalities*

A simple way to solve an inequality like this is to graph the equation $y = (x-3)(x-2)$ and see where $y < 0$.

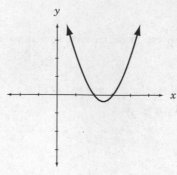

The graph indicates that $2 < x < 3$ are the only values of x for which $y < 0$, so choice (A) is correct. (B) is the wrong answer because it says y can be equal to 2 or 3. Since the inequality in the question says that y is less than but not equal to 0, $x \neq 3$ and $x \neq 2$.

22. (A) *Plane Geometry: Polygons; Statistics: Arithmetic Mean*

You can find the fifth angle of this polygon by subtracting the sum of the four other angles from the sum of all five angles. The formula for the sum of the interior angles in an n-sided polygon is $(n-2) \cdot 180°$. In this case $n = 5$, so the sum of the angles must be $540°$. The question gives you the average of 4 of the angles; this average will allow you to find the sum of those angles by using $\text{Average} = \dfrac{\text{Sum}}{\text{Number of Objects}}$. Since the average of the 4 angles is $120°$, the sum of the 4 angles is $480°$. You can find the fifth angle by subtracting this sum from the total: $\angle 5 = 540° - 480° = 60°$.

23. (B) *Algebra: Writing Equations*

You need to translate the statement into an algebraic expression. "The square of n plus n equals 2" translates into $n^2 + n = 2$. Now solve for n:

$$n^2 + n - 2 = 0$$
$$(n+2)(n-1) = 0$$
$$n = 1 \text{ or } n = -2$$

24. (E) *Algebra: Equation Solving*

Since $x^2 = y^2$, it may seem obvious to you that $x = y$, but you need to remember that the square of a number is always positive, even if the number itself is negative. For example, the square of 3 is equal to the square of -3. $x = -y$ is also a possible solution to this problem; thus the correct answer is (E).

25. (E) *Trigonometry: Pythagorean Identities*

This problem tests your knowledge of the trigonometric identity: $\sin^2 x + \cos^2 x = 1$. You should rearrange $\sin^2 \theta = \tan\theta - \cos^2\theta$ as:

$$\sin^2\theta + \cos^2\theta = \tan\theta$$
$$1 = \tan\theta$$

26. **(C)** *Plane Geometry: Polygons; Algebra: Writing Equations*

If you say that x is the length of the side of the square, then you can express the area of the square as $A = x^2$ and the perimeter as $P = 4x$. Since the sum of the area and the perimeter is 100, you can write the following algebraic expression:

$$x^2 + 4x = 100$$
$$x^2 + 4x - 100 = 0$$

Now apply the quadratic formula, $x = \dfrac{-b \pm \sqrt{b^2 - 4ac}}{2a}$, to find the value of x:

$$x = \frac{-4 \pm \sqrt{16 + 400}}{2}$$
$$x = \frac{-4 \pm \sqrt{416}}{2}$$
$$x = \frac{-4 \pm 20.4}{2}$$
$$= -12.2, 8.2$$

Since the side of the square can't have a negative length, the answer to this question is (C).

27. **(A)** *Functions: Compound Functions*

The question asks you for the value of $f(7)$ and tells you the value of $h(f(7))$. The simplest approach to this problem is to think of $f(7)$ not as a function but as a single entity. You can substitute $f(7)$ for x in the function $h(x) = 4x + 1$.

$$h(f(7)) = 4 \cdot f(7) + 1$$

The question tells you that $h(f(7)) = 13$, so you can solve for $f(7)$:

$$13 = 4 \cdot f(7) + 1$$
$$12 = 4 \cdot f(7)$$
$$3 = f(7)$$

28. **(D)** *Algebra: Equation Solving*

Whenever you see $x^2 - y^2$, you should factor it as $(x + y)(x - y)$, since it is a difference of squares. Usually, factoring $x^2 - y^2$ will reveal a simple solution to the problem.

$$x^2 - y^2 = 56$$
$$(x + y)(x - y) = 56$$

The question tells you that $x - y = 8$, so you can substitute 8 into the equation:

$$(x + y) \cdot 8 = 56$$
$$x + y = 7$$

If you perform equation addition on $x + y = 7$ and $x - y = 8$, you can eliminate y and obtain:

$$2x = 15$$
$$x = 7.5$$

Plug this value for x into one of the equations in order to find $y = -0.5$. Now you can solve for $\frac{x}{y}$:

$$\frac{x}{y} = \frac{7.5}{-0.5}$$
$$= -15$$

29. **(B)** *Plane Geometry: Triangles*

The sum of the exterior angles in any polygon is $360°$, so you can write the following equation:

$$x + 2x + 3x = 360°$$
$$6x = 360°$$
$$x = 60°$$

30. **(D)** *Coordinate Geometry: Lines and Distance*

You should solve this problem by using the midpoint formula, which states that the midpoint of a line segment has coordinates equal to the average of the coordinates of the endpoints. You can write the formula as $(x_m, y_m) = \left(\frac{x_1 + x_2}{2}, \frac{y_1 + y_2}{2}\right)$. The question gives you the coordinates of the midpoint and one of the endpoints of the line segment; you can plug these coordinates into the formula to find the other endpoint:

$$(0, 0) = \left(\frac{-1 + x_2}{2}, \frac{4 + y_2}{2}\right)$$

Break this formula into parts to solve separately for the x and y coordinates of the endpoint:

$$\frac{x_2 - 1}{2} = 0$$
$$x_2 - 1 = 0$$
$$x_2 = 1$$

And:

$$\frac{4 + y_2}{2} = 0$$
$$4 + y_2 = 0$$
$$y_2 = -4$$

The other endpoint of this line is $(1, -4)$.

31. **(E)** *Statistics: Arithmetic Mean*

You're given the average heights of two different sets of people and asked to calculate the average height of those two sets combined. Since one set contains 3 people and the other set contains 5, you cannot simply add the two averages together and divide by 2. Instead, you need to calculate the total average as $\frac{\text{Sum of Individual Heights}}{\text{Total Number of People}}$. To find the sum of heights for each group, multiply the average height by the number of people: $(\text{Total Number of People}) \cdot (\text{Average Height}) = \text{Sum of Individual Heights}$.

$$3 \cdot 70 = 210 = \text{Sum of the heights of the 3 people}$$
$$5 \cdot 66 = 330 = \text{Sum of the heights of the 5 people}$$

Add these numbers together to calculate the sum of the heights of the 8 people:

$$210 + 330 = 540$$

Now you can calculate the average height of the 8 people by dividing 540 by 8.

$$\frac{540}{8} = 67.5 \text{ inches}$$

32. **(C)** *Functions: Domain and Range*

Every once in a while, you'll be given the range of a function and asked to find its domain. The range stated in this question means that the value of the function is greater than or equal to 2 and less than or equal to 3. A simple way to calculate the domain of this function is to set $f(x_1) = 2$ and solve for x_1. Then repeat this process, setting $f(x_2) = 3$:

$$f(x_1) = 2$$
$$\frac{2x_1 + 5}{3} = 2$$
$$x_1 = \frac{1}{2}$$

And:

$$f(x_2) = 3$$
$$\frac{2x_2 + 5}{3} = 3$$
$$x_2 = 2$$

The domain of the function is all values of x between or equal to the values you just calculated for x_1 and x_2.

33. **(D)** *Functions: Graphs of Functions*

You're asked to find a portion of the graph of a compound function. Before running to your calculator, you first need to figure out the compound function. When you see a compound function, $f(h(x))$, you should plug the value of the interior function (in this case, $h(x) = x - 4$) into the exterior function (in this case, $f(x) = \sqrt{x}$).

$$f(h(x)) = f(x - 4)$$
$$= \sqrt{x - 4}$$

Now graph this function on your calculator.

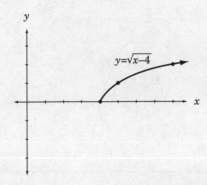

The correct answer choice is (D).

34. **(D)** *Plane Geometry: Polygons; Coordinate Geometry: Coordinate Plane*

Draw the three points you are given on a coordinate plane.

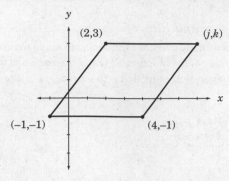

The four sides of a rhombus are of equal length, and opposing sides of a rhombus are parallel. The definition of a rhombus means that the distance between $(2, 3)$ and (j, k) must be the same as the distance between $(-1, -1)$ and $(4, -1)$. Since $(4, -1)$ is 5 steps to the right of $(-1, -1)$, then (j, k) must be 5 to the right of $(2, 3)$; therefore, (j, k) is the point $(7, 3)$.

35. **(E)** *Functions: Transformations and Symmetry*

You will inevitably encounter a question on "even" and "odd" functions on the Math IC, although you won't need to know this terminology in order to answer the question. If $f(-x) = -f(x)$, then f is an odd function. An odd function is symmetric through the origin, which is a fancy way of saying that, if the point $(x, f(x))$ is on the graph, then the point $(-x, -f(x))$ must be too. The expression simply indicates that when you plug $-x$ into $f(x)$, you make $f(x)$ negative. If $(2, 65)$ is on the graph, then the point $(-2, -65)$ must be too.

36. **(B)** *Functions: Graphs of Functions*

An efficient way to solve this problem is to use a graphing calculator. Graph the given function and set the window so the minimum and maximum x values are 0 and 5, respectively.

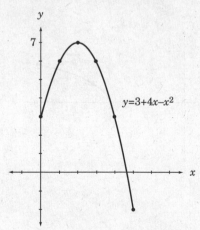

$y = 3 + 4x - x^2$

Usually a glance at the graph will help you eliminate obviously-wrong answer choices. You can see immediately that (C) and (D), for instance, cannot be correct because the graph goes above the x-axis. You can also see that (E) is incorrect because the graph does have a maximum value over this interval. Your calculator should have a function to find the maximum value, which is 7.

Alternatively, you can calculate the answer by hand, if you recognize that the equation is a parabola. The maximum value over this interval is the y-value of the vertex. Find the vertex of the parabola by completing the square to rewrite the equation:

$$f(x) = 3 + 4x - x^2$$
$$y = -x^2 + 4x + 3$$
$$y = -(x^2 - 4x) + 3$$
$$y - 4 = -(x^2 - 4x + 4) + 3$$
$$y = -(x - 2)^2 + 7$$

From this equation, you can see that the vertex is $(2, 7)$, and the y-coordinate of the vertex, 7, is the maximum value of the function.

37. **(B)** *Solid Geometry: Prisms*

The question asks you to solve for the volume of the cylinder in terms of its height, h. In order to find a right circular cylinder's volume, you need to know its radius r, in addition to its height, since volume is calculated as $V = \pi r^2 h$. Fortunately, the question tells you that the height of the cylinder is equal to twice the diameter, and you know that the diameter is twice the radius. If $h = 2d$, where d is the diameter, then $h = 4r$, where r is the radius of the cylinder. You can rewrite this expression to define the radius in terms of height: $r = \dfrac{h}{4}$. Now plug this information into the volume formula:

$$V = \pi r^2 h$$
$$= \pi \left(\frac{h}{4}\right)^2 h$$
$$= \pi \frac{h^2}{16} h$$
$$= \frac{\pi h^3}{16}$$

38. **(C)** *Algebra: Polynomials*

Before you try some complicated polynomial long division, see whether you can factor each of these polynomials. Factoring almost always reveals a simple solution to Math IC problems.

$$p(x) = 2 - x - x^2$$
$$= (2 + x)(1 - x)$$

And:

$$q(x) = x^2 - 3x + 2$$
$$= (x - 2)(x - 1)$$

Now you can divide $p(x)$ by $q(x)$:

$$\frac{q(x)}{p(x)} = \frac{(x - 2)(x - 1)}{(2 + x)(1 - x)}$$

$\dfrac{x-1}{1-x}$ cancels, leaving behind -1.

$$\frac{q(x)}{p(x)} = \frac{-(x-2)}{(2+x)}$$

$$= \frac{2-x}{2+x}$$

39. **(A)** *Trigonometry: Basic Functions, Word Problems*

When you encounter a word problem like this, try illustrating the problem:

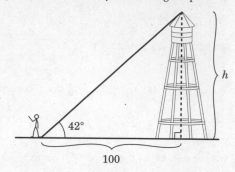

The picture shows the right triangle formed by John and the water tower has a base of 100 and a height equal to the height of the tower. Since you know that $\theta = 42°$, you can set up a basic trig problem to find the height of the tower: $\tan\theta = \dfrac{\text{Opposite}}{\text{Adjacent}}$, where the opposite is the height of the tower, and the adjacent is the distance of 100 feet to the tower.

$$\tan 42° = \frac{h}{100}$$

$$100 \tan 42° = h$$

$$90.04 = h$$

40. **(C)** *Solid Geometry: Solids that Aren't Prisms*

Your first step should be to visualize how the triangle turns into the cone:

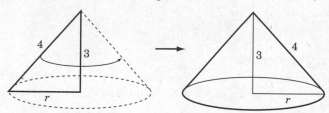

The question asks you to find the volume of the cone. Calculating the volume using the formula $V = \frac{1}{3}\pi r^2 h$ requires that you know the radius and the height of the cone. The height of the cone is given by the length BC. The radius of the revolved cone is given by the length of the third, or bottom, side of the triangle. Finding the cone's radius reduces to finding the triangle's bottom side. Use the Pythagorean Theorem to calculate the length of the side: $3^2 + r^2 = 4^2$, so $r^2 = 16 - 9$ and $r = \sqrt{7}$. Now you have all the materials to calculate the cone's volume:

$$V = \frac{1}{3}\pi r^2 h$$
$$= \frac{1}{3}\pi(\sqrt{7})^2 3$$
$$= \frac{1}{3}\pi 7 \cdot 3$$
$$= 7\pi$$

41. **(D)** *Plane Geometry: Polygons, Triangles*

The perimeter of a square with sides x is $4x$. The perimeter of an equilateral triangle with sides s is $3s$. The question states that the perimeters of the square and the triangle are equal, and you can express this as $4x = 3s$. In order to find the ratio of their areas, you need to know the formulas for their areas: the area of a square is x^2, and the area of an equilateral triangle is $\frac{\sqrt{3}}{4}s^2$. Because the ratios in the answer choices are given as numbers with no variables, you need to cancel the variables x and s out. The way to cancel them is to write both areas in terms of one variable. You have the expression $4x = 3s$, which you can turn into $x = \frac{3}{4}s$ (the side of the square is 3/4 the length of the side of the triangle). Plug this value for x into the formula for a square's area:

$$A_{square} = x^2$$
$$= \left(\frac{3}{4}s\right)^2$$
$$= \frac{9s^2}{16}$$

Now you have the square's area in terms of s. You also have the triangle's area in terms of s:

$$A_{eq\Delta} = \frac{\sqrt{3}}{4}s^2$$

Divide the area of the triangle by the area of the square to find the ratio:

$$\frac{A_{eq\Delta}}{A_{square}} = \frac{\frac{\sqrt{3}}{4}s^2}{\frac{9s^2}{16}}$$
$$= \frac{4\sqrt{3}}{9}$$

42. **(E)** *Functions: Compound Functions*

This compound function question is simpler than it seems. Since $g(f(x)) = x$ and since you want to solve for $g(7)$, you should set $f(x) = 7$ and solve for x.

$$f(x) = 7$$
$$2x - 5 = 7$$
$$2x = 12$$
$$x = 6$$

Since the question tells you that $g(f(x)) = x$, you know:

$$g(7) = 6$$

43. **(B)** *Fundamentals: Integers; Statistics: Probability*

Although you may think you need to do some division in order to solve this problem, you don't. Because the set of numbers involved in this question is infinite, you would spend the rest of your life dividing every number by 11 to see which ones leave an even remainder. Instead, everything you need to know is given to you in the question. The set of all possible remainders when dividing a positive integer by 11 is $\{0, 1, 2, 3, 4, 5, 6, 7, 8, 9, 10\}$ —11 possible remainders. Of these remainders, only $\{0, 2, 4, 6, 8, 10\}$—6 remainders—are even. The probability of an even remainder is given by:

$$P(\text{even remainder}) = \frac{\text{Number of Even Remainders}}{\text{Total Number of Remainders}}$$
$$= \frac{6}{11}$$

44. **(A)** *Algebra: Equation Solving, Word Problems*

This question sounds complicated because of the physics terms it uses (acceleration, velocity), but you don't need to know anything about physics to get this question right. As with many word problems, you should translate the problem into an algebraic expression. Use a to represent acceleration and v to represent velocity. The question states that a is directly proportional to v^2. "Directly proportional" does not mean that a and v^2 are equal, but it does mean that the ratio between them is constant. You can express the relationship algebraically as $a = K \cdot v^2$, where K is a constant. You can find K by plugging in 10 for the acceleration and 125 for the velocity:

$$a = K \cdot v^2$$
$$10 = K \cdot (125)^2$$
$$\frac{10}{15625} = K$$

Now you can solve for the acceleration when the velocity is equal to 150:

$$a = \frac{10}{15625} \cdot (150)^2$$
$$a = 14.4$$

45. **(C)** *Solid Geometry: Prisms*

The formula for the volume of a square with sides s is $V = s^3$. Since the question asks you to solve for the volume in terms of the long diagonal, you first need to find the cube's side in terms of the long diagonal. In the figure below, you can see how the sides of the cube relate to the diagonal:

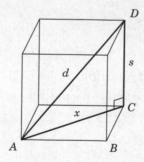

The diagonal of the base (x), the long diagonal (d), and the side (s) form a right triangle. You know that $x = \sqrt{2}s$, since $\triangle ABC$ is a 45-45-90 triangle with sides of length s and hypotenuse x:

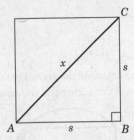

$\triangle ACD$ is a right triangle with sides s and $\sqrt{2}s$ and hypotenuse d. You can use the Pythagorean theorem to calculate d in terms of s:

$$d^2 = x^2 + s^2$$
$$= (\sqrt{2}s)^2 + s^2$$
$$= 2s^2 + s^2$$
$$= 3s^2$$
$$d = \sqrt{3}s$$
$$s = \frac{d}{\sqrt{3}}$$

Now you can plug this value for s into the volume formula:

$$V = s^3$$
$$= \left(\frac{d}{\sqrt{3}}\right)^3$$
$$= \frac{d^3}{3\sqrt{3}}$$
$$= \frac{\sqrt{3}d^3}{9}$$

46. (D) *Miscellaneous Math: Logic*

There is one rule of logic that you need to know for the Math IC: "if p, then q" is logically equivalent to its contrapositive "if *not q*, then *not p*." To find the contrapositive of a statement, reverse the order of the phrases and then put a "not" in front of each of them. In this case, "if the sun is shining, then the grass is dry" is equivalent to "if the grass is not dry, then the sun is not shining."

47. (E) *Trigonometry: Pythagorean Identities*

You should definitely memorize the Pythagorean identities because they will help you simplify seemingly complex trig expressions. This particular problem requires the identity $\sin^2 x + \cos^2 x = 1$. You might want to simplify the expressions $(\sin x + \cos x)^2$ and $(\sin x - \cos x)^2$ separately before you add them together:

$$(\sin x + \cos x)^2 = \sin^2 x + 2\sin x \cos x + \cos^2 x$$
$$= 2\sin x \cos x + 1$$

Similarly:

$$(\sin x - \cos x)^2 = \sin^2 x - 2\sin x \cos x + \cos^2 x$$
$$= 1 - 2\sin x \cos x$$

Now add the two parts together:

$$(\sin x + \cos x)^2 + (\sin x - \cos x)^2 = (2\sin x \cos x + 1) + (1 - 2\sin x \cos x)$$
$$= 1 + 1$$
$$= 2$$

48. **(A)**   *Plane Geometry: Circles, Polygons*

The easiest way to solve this problem is to calculate the area of the shaded region as the difference between the two areas you can easily find: the area of the sector and the area of the isosceles triangle.

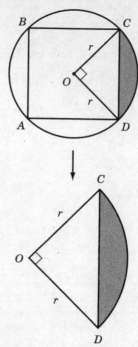

The area of $\triangle OCD$ is $\frac{1}{4}$ of the area of the square. The question tells you that the square has an area of 8, so this triangle has an area of 2.

The easiest way to calculate the area of sector OCD is to recognize that the sector's area is $\frac{1}{4}$ of the circle's area. To find the area of the circle, you need its radius r. To find r, use the formula for the area of a triangle, $A = \frac{1}{2}bh$, where the base and the height are both equal to r:

$$A_{\triangle OCD} = \frac{1}{2}(r \cdot r)$$
$$2 = \frac{r^2}{2}$$
$$4 = r^2$$
$$2 = r$$

Although mathematically r can be equal to -2, a negative radius doesn't make much sense. The formula for the area of a circle is $A = \pi r^2$; since the area of the sector is a quarter of the area of the circle, you can write:

$$\text{Sector } OCD = \frac{1}{4}\pi(2)^2$$
$$\text{Sector } OCD = \pi$$

Alternatively, you can find the area of the sector by using this formula: $A = \frac{n}{360} \cdot \pi r^2$, where n is the measure of the central angle that forms the sector. In this question n is $90°$, so you have:

$$A = \frac{90}{360} \cdot \pi (2)^2$$
$$= \frac{1}{4} \cdot \pi (4)$$
$$= \pi$$

To find the area of the shaded region, you should subtract the area of the triangle from the area of the sector: $\pi - 2 \approx 1.14$.

49. **(D)** *Plane Geometry: Triangles*

The figure in the question consists of three similar right triangles: the large triangle, $\triangle ABC$, and the two small triangles, $\triangle ADB$ and $\triangle BDC$.

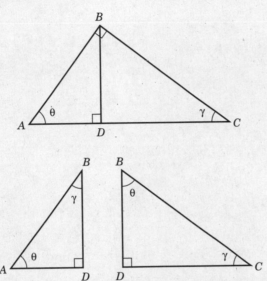

The small triangles, $\triangle ADB$ and $\triangle BDC$, are similar to the large triangle, $\triangle ABC$, which means that the ratio of the sides in each triangle is the same and that the angles in each triangle are the same. Because of the similarity, you know that $\angle DBA$ is γ and $\angle DBC$ is θ. In order to answer this question, you should set up a ratio for the triangles' sides. Because you're looking for the value of $(BD)^2$, your ratio should involve the two triangles that have the length BD: $\triangle ADB$ and $\triangle BDC$.

$$\frac{BD}{DC} = \frac{AD}{BD}$$

If you cross multiply this ratio, you get: $(BD)^2 = AD \cdot DC$.

$$\frac{AB}{AC} = \frac{AD}{AB}$$

So $AD \cdot DC = 36$.

50. (C) *Algebra: Equation Solving; Plane Geometry: Triangles*

$\triangle ABC$ is a right triangle, so $x + \frac{1}{x} = 90$, since the third angle (the right angle) in the triangle is equal to 90°.

$$\left(x + \frac{1}{x}\right)^2 = 90^2$$

$$\left(x + \frac{1}{x}\right) \cdot \left(x + \frac{1}{x}\right) = 8100$$

$$x^2 + 2 + \frac{1}{x^2} = 8100$$

$$x^2 + \frac{1}{x^2} = 8098$$

SAT II Math IC
Practice Test 3

MATH IC TEST 3 ANSWER SHEET

1. Ⓐ Ⓑ Ⓒ Ⓓ Ⓔ	18. Ⓐ Ⓑ Ⓒ Ⓓ Ⓔ	35. Ⓐ Ⓑ Ⓒ Ⓓ Ⓔ		
2. Ⓐ Ⓑ Ⓒ Ⓓ Ⓔ	19. Ⓐ Ⓑ Ⓒ Ⓓ Ⓔ	36. Ⓐ Ⓑ Ⓒ Ⓓ Ⓔ		
3. Ⓐ Ⓑ Ⓒ Ⓓ Ⓔ	20. Ⓐ Ⓑ Ⓒ Ⓓ Ⓔ	37. Ⓐ Ⓑ Ⓒ Ⓓ Ⓔ		
4. Ⓐ Ⓑ Ⓒ Ⓓ Ⓔ	21. Ⓐ Ⓑ Ⓒ Ⓓ Ⓔ	38. Ⓐ Ⓑ Ⓒ Ⓓ Ⓔ		
5. Ⓐ Ⓑ Ⓒ Ⓓ Ⓔ	22. Ⓐ Ⓑ Ⓒ Ⓓ Ⓔ	39. Ⓐ Ⓑ Ⓒ Ⓓ Ⓔ		
6. Ⓐ Ⓑ Ⓒ Ⓓ Ⓔ	23. Ⓐ Ⓑ Ⓒ Ⓓ Ⓔ	40. Ⓐ Ⓑ Ⓒ Ⓓ Ⓔ		
7. Ⓐ Ⓑ Ⓒ Ⓓ Ⓔ	24. Ⓐ Ⓑ Ⓒ Ⓓ Ⓔ	41. Ⓐ Ⓑ Ⓒ Ⓓ Ⓔ		
8. Ⓐ Ⓑ Ⓒ Ⓓ Ⓔ	25. Ⓐ Ⓑ Ⓒ Ⓓ Ⓔ	42. Ⓐ Ⓑ Ⓒ Ⓓ Ⓔ		
9. Ⓐ Ⓑ Ⓒ Ⓓ Ⓔ	26. Ⓐ Ⓑ Ⓒ Ⓓ Ⓔ	43. Ⓐ Ⓑ Ⓒ Ⓓ Ⓔ		
10. Ⓐ Ⓑ Ⓒ Ⓓ Ⓔ	27. Ⓐ Ⓑ Ⓒ Ⓓ Ⓔ	44. Ⓐ Ⓑ Ⓒ Ⓓ Ⓔ		
11. Ⓐ Ⓑ Ⓒ Ⓓ Ⓔ	28. Ⓐ Ⓑ Ⓒ Ⓓ Ⓔ	45. Ⓐ Ⓑ Ⓒ Ⓓ Ⓔ		
12. Ⓐ Ⓑ Ⓒ Ⓓ Ⓔ	29. Ⓐ Ⓑ Ⓒ Ⓓ Ⓔ	46. Ⓐ Ⓑ Ⓒ Ⓓ Ⓔ		
13. Ⓐ Ⓑ Ⓒ Ⓓ Ⓔ	30. Ⓐ Ⓑ Ⓒ Ⓓ Ⓔ	47. Ⓐ Ⓑ Ⓒ Ⓓ Ⓔ		
14. Ⓐ Ⓑ Ⓒ Ⓓ Ⓔ	31. Ⓐ Ⓑ Ⓒ Ⓓ Ⓔ	48. Ⓐ Ⓑ Ⓒ Ⓓ Ⓔ		
15. Ⓐ Ⓑ Ⓒ Ⓓ Ⓔ	32. Ⓐ Ⓑ Ⓒ Ⓓ Ⓔ	49. Ⓐ Ⓑ Ⓒ Ⓓ Ⓔ		
16. Ⓐ Ⓑ Ⓒ Ⓓ Ⓔ	33. Ⓐ Ⓑ Ⓒ Ⓓ Ⓔ	50. Ⓐ Ⓑ Ⓒ Ⓓ Ⓔ		
17. Ⓐ Ⓑ Ⓒ Ⓓ Ⓔ	34. Ⓐ Ⓑ Ⓒ Ⓓ Ⓔ			

REFERENCE INFORMATION

THE FOLLOWING INFORMATION IS FOR YOUR REFERENCE IN ANSWERING SOME OF THE QUESTIONS IN THIS TEST:

Volume of a right circular cone with radius r and height h: $V = \frac{1}{3}\pi r^2 h$

Lateral area of a right circular cone with circumference of the base c and slaight height ℓ: $S = \frac{1}{2}c\ell$

Volume of a sphere with radius r: $V = \frac{4}{3}\pi r^3$

Surface area of a sphere with radius r: $S = 4\pi r^2$

Volume of a pyramid with base area B and height h: $V = \frac{1}{3}Bh$

MATHEMATICS LEVEL IC TEST

For each of the following problems, decide which is the BEST of the choices given. If the exact numerical value is not one of the choices, select the choice that best approximates this value. Then fill in the corresponding oval on the answer sheet.

<u>Notes:</u> (1) A calculator will be necessary for answering some (but not all) of the questions in this test. For each question you will have to decide whether or not you should use a calcuator. The calculator you use must be at least a scientific calculator; programmable calculators and calculators that can display graphs are permitted.

(2) For some questions in this test you may need to decide whether your calculator should be in radian or degree mode.

(3) Figures that accompany problems in this test are intended to provide information useful in solving the problems. They are drawn as accurately as possible EXCEPT when it is stated in a specific problem that its figure is not drawn to scale. All figures lie in a plane unless otherwise indicated.

(4) Unless otherwise specified, the domain of any function f is assumed to be the set of all real numbers x for which $f(x)$ is a real number.

(5) Reference information that may be useful in answering the questions in this test can be found on the page preceding Question 1.

USE THIS SPACE FOR SCRATCHWORK.

1. If $\dfrac{3}{5-x} = \dfrac{1}{x-2}$, then $x =$

(A) $\dfrac{11}{4}$

(B) $\dfrac{5}{2}$

(C) 2

(D) $\dfrac{3}{2}$

(E) 1

2. If $\dfrac{1}{R} = \dfrac{1}{x} + \dfrac{1}{y}$, then $R =$

(A) $x^2 - y^2$

(B) $x^2 + y^2$

(C) $\dfrac{xy}{x+y}$

(D) $\dfrac{x+y}{xy}$

(E) $x + y$

GO ON TO THE NEXT PAGE

USE THIS SPACE FOR SCRATCHWORK.

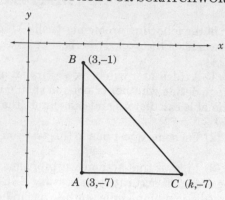

Figure 1

3. In Figure 1, if $\triangle ABC$ is an isosceles right triangle, what is the value of k ?

   (A) −9
   (B) −7
   (C) 7
   (D) 9
   (E) 10

4. If $f(x) = \dfrac{x+1}{x-2}$, what is the value of $f(3)$?

   (A) 5
   (B) 4
   (C) 2
   (D) 1
   (E) −1

5. If $z = x^2$ and $x = 4j$, what is the value of z when $j = 3$?

   (A) $\dfrac{9}{16}$

   (B) 25

   (C) 81

   (D) 144

   (E) 169

6. If $24^n = 2^4 \cdot 6^2$, then $n =$

   (A) 6
   (B) 5
   (C) 4
   (D) 3
   (E) 2

7. In Figure 2, line l is parallel to line m. What is the value of z?

   (A) $180 - x - y$
   (B) $x + y$
   (C) $180 + x + y$
   (D) $x + y - 180$
   (E) 180

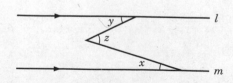

Figure 2

GO ON TO THE NEXT PAGE

8. At what point does the line $y = \frac{3}{4}x - 6$ intersect the x-axis?

(A) $x = 8$
(B) $x = 0$
(C) $x = 6$
(D) $x = -2$
(E) $y = 6$

9. A number n is decreased by 1. If the square root of that result equals $\frac{5}{4}$, what is the value of n?

(A) $\frac{40}{16}$

(B) $\frac{41}{16}$

(C) $\frac{39}{27}$

(D) $\frac{25}{16}$

(E) $\frac{3}{5}$

10. If $2x - 3y = 7$ and $3x - 2y = 5$, then $x =$

(A) $\frac{35}{2}$

(B) 5

(C) $\frac{1}{2}$

(D) $\frac{1}{5}$

(E) 0

11. The measures of the 4 interior angles of a quadrilateral are in a ratio of $1:2:3:4$. What is the measure, in degrees, of the largest angle?

(A) $36°$
(B) $120°$
(C) $144°$
(D) $148°$
(E) $160°$

GO ON TO THE NEXT PAGE

12. If the minute hand on a clock starts at 12:00 and rotates clockwise through an angle of 120°, on which number does the minute hand stop?

    (A) 4
    (B) 5
    (C) 6
    (D) 8
    (E) 9

13. If $f(x) = 3x^3 + 7x^2 + 2x + 1$, what is the value of $f(6.1)$?

    (A) 161.8
    (B) 221.7
    (C) 430.8
    (D) 433.7
    (E) 631.9

14. $x + y = 12$ and $x - y = 16$, then $\frac{x}{y} =$

    (A) −7

    (B) −6

    (C) 0

    (D) $\frac{1}{7}$

    (E) 7

15. The perimeter of a rectangle is 36, and its area is 72. What is the length of the rectangle's longer side?

    (A) 6
    (B) 8
    (C) 11
    (D) 12
    (E) 14

16. Which of the following is the solution to $|x - 3| \leq 3$?

    (A) $-3 \leq x \leq 3$
    (B) $0 < x < 6$
    (C) $0 \leq x \leq 6$
    (D) $-3 < x < 3$
    (E) $0 \leq x \leq 3$

GO ON TO THE NEXT PAGE

17. In Figure 3, if chord $\overline{AB}$ = chord $\overline{CD}$, then which of the following must be true?

   I. Arc $\overset{\frown}{AC}$ = Arc $\overset{\frown}{BD}$
   II. Arc $\overset{\frown}{CB}$ = $\frac{1}{2}$ Arc $\overset{\frown}{APD}$
   III. $\angle BAD \cong \angle CDA$

   (A) I only
   (B) II only
   (C) I and II only
   (D) I and III only
   (E) I, II, and III

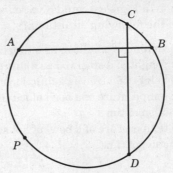

Note: Figure not drawn to scale.
Figure 3

18. There are 20 students in a room. 14 of the students have brown eyes, and 12 have blond hair. If a student is chosen randomly, what is the probability that he or she will have brown eyes <u>and</u> blond hair?

   (A) $\frac{1}{5}$

   (B) $\frac{3}{10}$

   (C) $\frac{2}{5}$

   (D) $\frac{7}{20}$

   (E) $\frac{3}{5}$

19. If $\log_b a = x$, which of the following must be true?

   (A) $b^x = a$
   (B) $a^x = b$
   (C) $a^b = x$
   (D) $x^b = a$
   (E) $x^a = b$

GO ON TO THE NEXT PAGE

20. The graph in Figure 4 could be a reasonable interpretation of which of the following situations?

    (A) The volume of a balloon as a function of the radius
    (B) The weight of a steel rod as a function of the radius
    (C) The height of a tree as a function of time
    (D) The temperature of a bowl of ice cream left on a table as a function of time
    (E) The temperature of a bowl of hot soup left on a table as a function of time

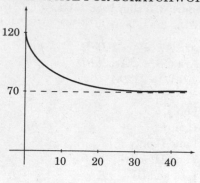

Figure 4

21. If a and b are real numbers, $i^2 = -1$, and $(2a - b) + 3i = 4 + ai$, then what is the value of b?

    (A) 4
    (B) 3
    (C) 2
    (D) $2 + i$
    (E) $2 - i$

22. John has 5 different history books in his library. If he puts 3 of them on a shelf, how many different arrangements are possible?

    (A) 122
    (B) 120
    (C) 90
    (D) 80
    (E) 60

23. In Figure 5, what is the value of $\cos \angle ABC$?

    (A) $\dfrac{5}{12}$

    (B) $\dfrac{12}{13}$

    (C) $\dfrac{5}{13}$

    (D) $\dfrac{15}{12}$

    (E) $\dfrac{7}{8}$

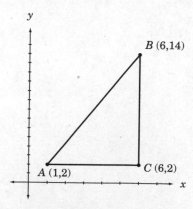

Figure 5

GO ON TO THE NEXT PAGE

24. A circle of radius 6 rolls without slipping for a distance of 700π. How many <u>complete</u> revolutions does the circle make?

    (A) 63
    (B) 62
    (C) 61
    (D) 59
    (E) 58

25. In Figure 6, what is the area of the shaded region?

    (A) 1.5
    (B) 1.67
    (C) 1.89
    (D) 2
    (E) 2.01

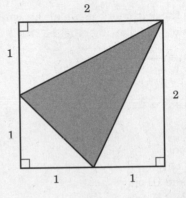

Figure 6

26. What is the distance between the points $(-6, -9)$ and $(12, 15)$?

    (A) 28.75
    (B) 29
    (C) 30
    (D) 30.18
    (E) 31.18

GO ON TO THE NEXT PAGE

27. Which of the following has the least value?

USE THIS SPACE FOR SCRATCHWORK.

    (A) 10^{-100}
    (B) $(-10)^{-100}$
    (C) $(-10)^{100}$
    (D) $(-10)^{101}$
    (E) $(-10)^{102}$

28. If A is the arithmetic mean of the real numbers x, y, and z, which of the following <u>must</u> be true?

    I. $A = \dfrac{x+y+z}{3}$

    II. $(A-x)+(A-y)+(A-z) = 0$

    III. $A+3 = \dfrac{x+y+z+3}{3}$

    (A) I only
    (B) II only
    (C) I and III only
    (D) I and II only
    (E) I, II, and III

29. A useful approximation for the exponential function e^x is given by the polynomial $1 + x + \dfrac{x^2}{2} + \dfrac{x^3}{6}$. <u>Using this polynomial</u>, find an approximation of e^1.

    (A) $\dfrac{271}{100}$

    (B) $\dfrac{8}{3}$

    (C) $\dfrac{9}{4}$

    (D) $\dfrac{11}{5}$

    (E) 2

GO ON TO THE NEXT PAGE

USE THIS SPACE FOR SCRATCHWORK.

30. A rectangle has sides of length 7 and 8, as shown in Figure 7. What is the value of $\angle CAD$?

    (A) 37.8°
    (B) 38.7°
    (C) 40.9°
    (D) 41.0°
    (E) 41.2°

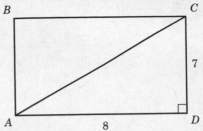

Note: Figure not drawn to scale.

Figure 7

31. If P and Q are two points on a cube with sides of length 10, then the maximum straight line distance between P and Q is

    (A) 17.3
    (B) 16.9
    (C) 16.8
    (D) 15.1
    (E) 12.7

32. If $f(x) = 6x - 7$ for all real x, then the slope of the line given by $y = f(3 - x)$ is

    (A) 6
    (B) 0
    (C) −1
    (D) −6
    (E) −7

33. In Figure 8, what is the value of x?

    (A) 3.2
    (B) 3.6
    (C) 3.8
    (D) 4.0
    (E) 4.4

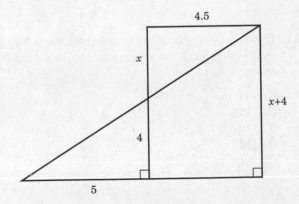

Note: Figure not drawn to scale.

Figure 8

GO ON TO THE NEXT PAGE

34. $\left(\dfrac{2}{\sin^2\theta + \cos^2\theta - 4}\right)^2 =$

    USE THIS SPACE FOR SCRATCHWORK.

    (A) -1

    (B) $-\dfrac{4}{9}$

    (C) $\dfrac{4}{9}$

    (D) $\dfrac{1}{2}$

    (E) 3

35. Given $6x^2 - 18x + 7 = 0$, if the sum of the roots is S and the product of the roots is P, then $S - P =$

    (A) $-\dfrac{29}{6}$

    (B) $-\dfrac{25}{6}$

    (C) -4

    (D) 0

    (E) $\dfrac{11}{6}$

36. If the measure of one angle in a rhombus is $72°$, and if the sides in the rhombus have a length of 12, then what is the area of the rhombus?

    (A) 44
    (B) 136
    (C) 137
    (D) 139
    (E) 140

37. A shirt cost $8.00 in 1970. Assuming a 6% rate of inflation, how much should the same shirt cost in 2003?

    (A) $55.61
    (B) $54.72
    (C) $54.26
    (D) $54.01
    (E) $53.98

GO ON TO THE NEXT PAGE

USE THIS SPACE FOR SCRATCHWORK.

38. For which of the following graphs does $f(-x) = -f(x)$?

(A)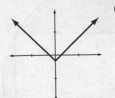

(B)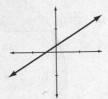

(C)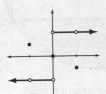

(D)

(E)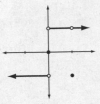

39. In quadrilateral $ABCD, AB = 2, BC = 4,$ and $CD = 5.$ Which of the following represents all possible values for AD?

(A) $0 < AD < 11$
(B) $0 \leq AD \leq 11$
(C) $1 \leq AD < 11$
(D) $1 < AD \leq 7$
(E) $0 < AD < 7$

40. How are the graphs of $y_1 = x + 2$ and $y_2 = \dfrac{x^2 - 4}{x - 2}$ related?

(A) They are different except when $x = 2.$
(B) They are totally different.
(C) They are exactly the same.
(D) They are the same except at $x = 2.$
(E) They are the same except at $x = -2.$

GO ON TO THE NEXT PAGE

41. Rectangle *ABCD* is inscribed in a circle as shown in Figure 9. If the length of side *AB* is 18 and the length of side *BC* is 24, what is the area of the shaded region?

    (A) 289.9
    (B) 288.0
    (C) 280.2
    (D) 275.1
    (E) 274.9

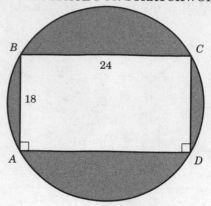

Note: Figure not drawn to scale.

Figure 9

42. If $f(x) = 3 - x^3$ and if f^{-1} is the inverse function of f, then what is $f^{-1}(7)$?

    (A) −1.59
    (B) −1.21
    (C) −0.19
    (D) 1.59
    (E) 2.13

43. If $f(x) = x + 3$ and $g(x) = \sqrt{x}$, which of the following is the range of $y = f(g(x))$?

    (A) $0 \le y$
    (B) $y \le 3$
    (C) $3 \le y$
    (D) $y \le 0$
    (E) $0 < y < 3$

44. Sequential arrangements of dots are formed according to a pattern. Each arrangement after the first is formed by adding another layer to the bottom of the pentagon, as shown in Figure 10. If this pattern continues, which of the following is the number of dots in the 4th arrangement?

    (A) 36
    (B) 35
    (C) 34
    (D) 33
    (E) 32

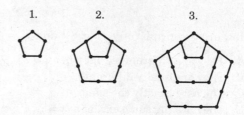

Figure 10

GO ON TO THE NEXT PAGE

45. The volume of a circular cylinder varies directly with the height of the cylinder and with the square of the cylinder's radius. If the height is halved and the radius is doubled, then the volume will be

   (A) unchanged
   (B) quadrupled
   (C) tripled
   (D) doubled
   (E) halved

46. Let $x \lozenge y$ is defined for pairs of positive integers as $x \lozenge y = \dfrac{x-y}{xy}$.
    If $x \lozenge y \geq 0$, then x and y could satisfy which of the following?

      I. $x = y$
     II. $x < y$
    III. $x > y$

   (A) I only
   (B) II only
   (C) III only
   (D) I and III only
   (E) I, II, and III

47. A laundry bag contains 160 black socks and 300 red socks. How many black socks must be added so that the probability of choosing a black sock is $\dfrac{7}{8}$?

   (A) 12
   (B) 13
   (C) 820
   (D) 1939
   (E) 1940

48. If the surfaces of two spheres S and T with radii 7 and 12, respectively, intersect at one point only, then the distance between the center of sphere S and the center of sphere T is

   (A) 19
   (B) 18
   (C) 17
   (D) 5
   (E) Not enough information to tell

GO ON TO THE NEXT PAGE

49. The faces of the front, side, and bottom of a rectangular solid have areas of 15 square feet, 7 square feet, and 4.2 square feet, respectively. What is the volume of this solid?

    (A) 21
    (B) 22
    (C) 441
    (D) 607
    (E) Not enough information to tell

50. If the lateral surface area S of the right circular cone in Figure 11 is twice the area of the cone's base, what is the cone's height h in terms of the radius r?

    (A) $\sqrt{2}r$
    (B) $\sqrt{3}r$
    (C) πr
    (D) $\sqrt{5}r$
    (E) $\sqrt{7}r$

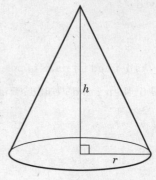

Figure 11

S T O P

IF YOU FINISH BEFORE TIME IS CALLED, YOU MAY CHECK YOUR WORK ON THIS TEST ONLY.
DO NOT TURN TO ANY OTHER TEST IN THIS BOOK.

SAT II Math IC
Practice Test 3
Explanations

Calculating Your Score

Question Number	Correct Answer	Right	Wrong	Question Number	Correct Answer	Right	Wrong	Question Number	Correct Answer	Right	Wrong
1.	A	___	___	18.	B	___	___	35.	E	___	___
2.	C	___	___	19.	A	___	___	36.	C	___	___
3.	D	___	___	20.	E	___	___	37.	B	___	___
4.	B	___	___	21.	C	___	___	38.	C	___	___
5.	D	___	___	22.	E	___	___	39.	A	___	___
6.	E	___	___	23.	B	___	___	40.	D	___	___
7.	B	___	___	24.	E	___	___	41.	E	___	___
8.	A	___	___	25.	A	___	___	42.	A	___	___
9.	B	___	___	26.	C	___	___	43.	C	___	___
10.	D	___	___	27.	D	___	___	44.	B	___	___
11.	C	___	___	28.	D	___	___	45.	D	___	___
12.	A	___	___	29.	B	___	___	46.	D	___	___
13.	D	___	___	30.	E	___	___	47.	E	___	___
14.	A	___	___	31.	A	___	___	48.	E	___	___
15.	D	___	___	32.	D	___	___	49.	A	___	___
16.	C	___	___	33.	B	___	___	50.	B	___	___
17.	D	___	___	34.	C	___	___				

Your raw score for the SAT II Math IC test is calculated from the number of questions you answer correctly and incorrectly. Once you have determined your composite score, use the conversion table on page 18 of this book to calculate your scaled score. To calculate your raw score, count the number of questions you answered correctly: _____

A

Count the number of questions you answered incorrectly, and multiply that number by $\frac{1}{4}$:

_____ × $\frac{1}{4}$ = _____

B C

Subtract the value in field C from value in field A: _____

D

Round the number in field D to the nearest whole number. This is your raw score: _____

E

Test 3 Explanations

Math IC Test 3 Explanations

1. **(A)** *Algebra: Equation Solving*

Because x is in the denominators of the two fractions, you should cross multiply to simplify this equation.

$$\frac{3}{5-x} = \frac{1}{x-2}$$
$$3x - 6 = 5 - x$$
$$4x = 11$$
$$x = \frac{11}{4}$$

2. **(C)** *Algebra: Algebraic Manipulation*

If you invert both sides of the equation $\frac{1}{R} = \frac{1}{x} + \frac{1}{y}$, then you get $R = \dfrac{1}{\frac{1}{x} + \frac{1}{y}}$. The common denominator of $\frac{1}{x}$ and $\frac{1}{y}$ is xy.

$$R = \frac{1}{\frac{1}{x}\left(\frac{y}{y}\right) + \frac{1}{y}\left(\frac{x}{x}\right)}$$
$$= \frac{1}{\frac{y}{xy} + \frac{x}{xy}}$$
$$= \frac{1}{\frac{y+x}{xy}}$$
$$= \frac{xy}{y+x}$$

3. **(D)** *Coordinate Geometry: Coordinate Plane; Plane Geometry: Triangles*

The question tells you that $\triangle ABC$ is a right isosceles triangle, which means that the legs of the triangle, AB and AC, are equal in length. You can find the length of the legs by using the coordinates of points A, B, and C. The length of AB is equal to the difference in the y-coordinates of A and B: $(-1) - (-7) = 6$. The length of AC is equal the difference in the x-coordinates of A and C: $k - 3$. Since $AB = AC$, you know that $k - 3 = 6$ and $k = 9$.

4. **(B)** *Functions: Evaluating Functions*

Plug in 3 for x in $f(x)$:

$$f(3) = \frac{3+1}{3-2}$$
$$= \frac{4}{1}$$
$$= 4$$

5. **(D)** *Functions: Evaluating Functions*

You can solve this problem through substitution. If $j = 3$, then $x = 4 \times 3 = 12$. If $x = 12$, then $z = 12^2 = 144$.

6. (E) *Fundamentals: Exponents*

To answer this question you need to know the following laws of exponents: $A^x \cdot B^x = (AB)^x$ and $(A^x)^y = A^{xy}$. You should apply these laws to the problem given in the question: $24^n = 2^4 \cdot 6^2$. Rewrite 2^4 as $(2^2)^2$, which you can simplify to 4^2. Now you have:

$$24^n = 4^2 \cdot 6^2$$
$$= (4 \cdot 6)^2$$
$$24^n = 24^2$$
$$n = 2$$

7. (B) *Plane Geometry: Lines and Angles*

Try redrawing the figure like this:

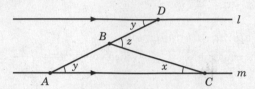

By extending the line BD to point A, you can see that BD is part of a transversal intersecting two parallel lines. When two parallel lines are cut by a transversal, the alternate interior angles $\angle y$ and $\angle CAB$ are equal to each other. By extending BD, you also create a triangle $\triangle ABC$, with two angles: $\angle y$ and $\angle x$. The third angle, $\angle ABC$, is supplementary to $\angle z$. In other words, the two angles add up to $180°$. Since $\angle z + \angle ABC = 180°$ and $\angle x + \angle y + \angle ABC = 180°$, you can see that $\angle z = \angle x + \angle y$.

8. (A) *Coordinate Geometry: Lines; Algebra: Equation Solving*

When a line intersects the x-axis, the value of y is zero. So you can find the x-intercept of the line by plugging in $y = 0$.

$$y = \frac{3}{4}x - 6$$
$$0 = \frac{3}{4}x - 6$$
$$\frac{3}{4}x = 6$$
$$x = 8$$

9. (B) *Algebra: Writing Equations*

Translate the problem into an algebraic expression. "A number n is decreased by 1" means the same thing as $(n-1)$. You can write "the square root of that result equals $\frac{5}{4}$" as $\sqrt{n-1} = \frac{5}{4}$. Now solve for n. Start by squaring both sides of the equation.

$$\sqrt{n-1} = \frac{5}{4}$$
$$n - 1 = \frac{25}{16}$$
$$n = \frac{25}{16} + 1$$
$$n = \frac{41}{16}$$

10. **(D)**   *Algebra: Systems of Equations*

You have two unknown variables and two equations. In order to solve for x, you need x to be the only variable in an equation. The easiest way to isolate x is to use substitution: solve for y in terms of x in one equation, and then plug that value for y into the second equation to find x.

$$3x - 2y = 5$$
$$2y = 3x - 5$$
$$y = \frac{3x - 5}{2}$$

Now plug this value for y into the other equation and solve for x:

$$2x - 3y = 7$$
$$2x - 3\left(\frac{3x - 5}{2}\right) = 7$$
$$2x - \frac{9x - 15}{2} = 7$$
$$4x - 9x + 15 = 14$$
$$-5x = -1$$
$$x = \frac{1}{5}$$

11. **(C)**   *Algebra: Writing Equations; Plane Geometry: Polygons*

The sum of the interior angles in a quadrilateral is $360°$. If you make x the measure of the smallest angle in the quadrilaterial, you can set up an equation for the angles by using the ratio given in the question.

$$360° = x + 2x + 3x + 4x$$
$$= 10x$$
$$x = 36°$$

The largest angle in the quadrilaterial is equal to $4x$, or $4 \cdot 36° = 144°$.

12. **(A)**   *Coordinate Geometry: Circles, Word Problems*

If the minute hand starts at 12:00 and rotates $120°$, it has traveled $\frac{120°}{360°} = \frac{1}{3}$ of the way around the full circle (since there are $360°$ in a circle). Since there are 12 hours (at even intervals) on a clock, $\frac{1}{3}$ of the circle represents $\left(\frac{1}{3} \cdot 12\right)$ hours, or 4 hours. Since the hand starts at 12:00, it ends up pointing at 4:00.

13. **(D)**   *Functions: Evaluating Functions*

Plug 6.1 into $f(x)$, and figure out the answer on your calculator.

$$f(6.1) = 3(6.1)^3 - 7(6.1)^2 + 2(6.1) + 1$$
$$= 3 \cdot (226.981) - 7(37.21) + 12.2 + 1$$
$$= 680.943 - 260.47 + 13.2$$
$$\approx 433.7$$

14. **(A)**   *Algebra: Systems of Equations*

The fastest way to answer this problem is to add together the equations $x + y = 12$ and $x - y = 16$. Once you add the equations, the y terms cancel out, and you end up with $2x = 28$. Now you can find that $x = 14$. If you plug $x = 14$ into one of the original equations, such as $x + y = 12$, you'll find that $y = -2$. To answer the problem, divide x by y: $\dfrac{x}{y} = \dfrac{14}{-2} = -7$.

15. **(D)**   *Plane Geometry: Polygons*

Draw a picture of the rectangle, labeling the long sides y and the short sides x.

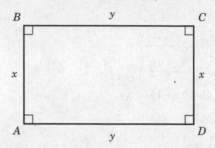

The perimeter of $\square ABCD$ is 36. You know that the perimeter of a polygon is the sum of its sides, so you can write $2x + 2y = 36$, or $x + y = 18$. Since you have two unknown variables, you need to write a second equation. The area of $\square ABCD$ is 72. You calculate the area of a rectangle by multiplying its short side by its long side, so you have $xy = 72$. Rewrite the first equation as $y = 18 - x$ and substitute this value for y into the second equation:

$$x \cdot y = 72$$
$$x(18 - x) = 72$$
$$18x - x^2 = 72$$
$$x^2 - 18x + 72 = 0$$
$$(x - 6)(x - 12) = 0$$
$$x = 6 \text{ or } x = 12$$

Since 12 is greater than 6, 12 is the length of the rectangle's long side.

16. **(C)**   *Algebra: Inequalities, Absolute Value*

When you see an inequality with an absolute value on one side, you're actually dealing with two inequalities. $|x - 3| \le 3$ can be rewritten as $x - 3 \le 3$ and $x - 3 \ge -3$. First, solve these inequalities separately:

$$x - 3 \le 3$$
$$x \le 6$$

And:

$$x - 3 \ge -3$$
$$x \ge 0$$

You can rewrite these two inequalities as $0 \le x \le 6$.

17. **(D)** *Plane Geometry: Circles*

In a circle, chords of equal length intercept arcs of equal length, so $\overarc{AB} = \overarc{CD}$. You can also see from the figure that $\overarc{AC} + \overarc{CB} = \overarc{AB}$ and $\overarc{BD} + \overarc{CB} = \overarc{CD}$. Now you can write:

$$\overarc{AC} + \overarc{CB} = \overarc{BD} + \overarc{CB}$$
$$\overarc{AC} = \overarc{BD}$$

So Option I must be true.

Option III must also be true. If $\overarc{AB} = \overarc{CD}$, then $\angle BAD \cong \angle CDA$ because the angles intersect arcs of equal length.

Option II is not necessarily true, though. For instance, if both AB and CD were diameters of the circle, then points A, B, C, and D would divide the circle into four equal arcs:

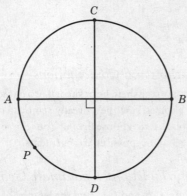

As you can see in the figure above, $\overarc{CB} = \overarc{APD}$, so option II, which says $\overarc{CB} = \frac{1}{2}\overarc{APD}$, cannot be true.

18. **(B)** *Statistics: Probability*

You can draw a Venn diagram to help you answer this problem.

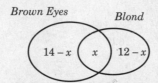

x is the number of brown-eyed, blond students. $12 - x$ is the number of blond students without brown eyes, and $14 - x$ is the number of brown-eyed students without blond hair. The total amount of students is $(12 - x) + x + (14 - x) = 26 - x$. Since the question says that there are 20 students total, you can solve for x: $26 - x = 20$, so $x = 6$. Since x is the number of students with brown eyes and blond hair, you can calculate the probability of choosing one of these students by dividing 6 by 20 to get $\frac{3}{10}$.

19. **(A)** *Fundamentals: Logarithms*

This problem asks you for the definition of a logarithm, which you should definitely memorize for the Math IC. $\log_b a = x$ is equivalent to $b^x = a$.

20. **(E)** *Functions: Graphs of Functions*

You need to interpret the graph and apply your interpretation to the answer choices. The graph shows a y value that starts at 120 and decreases to 70, where it remains constant as the x value increases. Of the answer choices, this graph best represents choice (E), since a bowl of hot soup left out on a table would cool to room temperature over time, and it would stay at room temperature as time passed.

21. **(C)** *Algebra: Equation Solving, Complex Numbers*

This equation has both a real and a complex component. In order to solve the equation, you first need to equate the complex components. If $(2a - b) + 3i = 4 + ai$, then the complex part of the equation states $3i = ai$, so $a = 3$. Now you can equate the real components: if $2a - b = 4$ and $a = 3$, then:

$$2a - b = 4$$
$$6 - b = 4$$
$$b = 2$$

22. **(E)** *Statistics: Permutations and Combinations*

When John picks the first book to put on the shelf, he has a total of 5 choices (since there are 5 books). When he picks the second book, he has 4 choices, since he's already removed one of the books. Finally, when he makes his third pick, he has 3 books to choose from. You can calculate the number of possible arrangements by multiplying $5 \cdot 4 \cdot 3 = 60$ possible arrangements.

23. **(B)** *Trigonometry: Basic Functions; Coordinate Geometry: Coordinate Plane*

You can use the coordinates of points A, B, and C to find the lengths of the sides of $\triangle ABC$. The length of AC is equal to the difference between the x-coordinates of points A and C: $6 - 1 = 5$. The length of BC is equal to the difference between the y-coordinates of B and C: $14 - 2 = 12$. Now that you have the two legs of the triangle, you can figure out its hypotenuse. A right triangle with two legs of lengths 5 and 12 must have a hypotenuse of 13 (it's a special right triangle). If you don't remember this special triangle, you can use the Pythagorean theorem to find AB:

$$(AB)^2 = 5^2 + 12^2$$
$$= 169$$
$$AB = 13$$

Now you can solve $\cos \angle ABC$, since BC is the adjacent side to the angle and AB is the hypotenuse of the triangle:

$$\cos \angle ABC = \frac{BC}{AB}$$
$$= \frac{12}{13}$$

24. **(E)** *Plane Geometry: Circles*

The distance a circle rolls in one complete revolution is equal to the circle's circumference. If the radius of a circle is 6, then the circumference of the circle is 12π, since $C = 2\pi r$. You can find the number of revolutions the circle makes by dividing the total distance by the circumference:

$$\text{number of revolutions} = \frac{\text{total distance}}{\text{circumference}}$$

$$= \frac{700\pi}{12\pi}$$

$$= 58\frac{1}{3}$$

Since the question asks you for the number of revolutions completed by the circle, the correct answer is 58.

25. **(A)** *Plane Geometry: Polygons, Triangles*

You'll waste a lot of time trying to calculate the area of the triangle by figuring out the length of the base and the height. The fastest way to answer this problem is to subtract the unshaded area from the area of the whole figure. The area of the whole figure is the area of the square $\square ABCD$. You can calculate the square's area by multiplying its sides together: Area $\square ABCD = 2 \cdot 2 = 4$. The unshaded area consists of three right triangles:

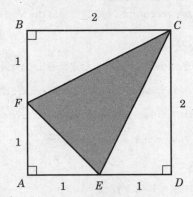

The figure in the question gives you the bases and heights of these three triangles, so you can calculate their areas:

$$\text{Area } \Delta AFE = \frac{1}{2}(1)(1) = \frac{1}{2}$$

$$\text{Area } \Delta FBC = \frac{1}{2}(1)(2) = 1$$

$$\text{Area } \Delta ECD = \frac{1}{2}(1)(2) = 1$$

Add the areas of the three triangles together to find the unshaded area: $\frac{1}{2} + 1 + 1 = 2\frac{1}{2}$. You can find the area of the shaded triangle by subtracting the unshaded area from the total area:

$$4 - 2\frac{1}{2} = 1\frac{1}{2} = 1.5$$

26. **(C)** *Coordinate Geometry: Lines and Distance*

You should definitely memorize the formula for finding the distance between two points in a plane. If you have two points (x_1, y_1) and (x_2, y_2), then the distance formula is: $d = \sqrt{(x_2 - x_1)^2 + (y_2 - y_1)^2}$. Plug the points $(-6, -9)$ and $(12, 15)$ into this formula:

$$
\begin{aligned}
d &= \sqrt{(12 - (-6))^2 + (15 - (-9))^2} \\
&= \sqrt{18^2 + 24^2} \\
&= \sqrt{900} \\
&= 30
\end{aligned}
$$

27. **(D)** *Fundamentals: Exponents*

The answer choices are probably too large for your calculator to compute, so you should figure out their values on your own. 10^{-100} is an extremely small positive number; your calculator will probably say it's equal to zero. $(-10)^{-100}$ is equal to 10^{-100}, since the exponent is an even number. (If you don't understand why this is true, try replacing 10 and 100 with smaller numbers: $(-2)^{-2} = 0.25$ and $2^{-2} = 0.25$.) $(-10)^{100}$ is a very large positive number—in fact, it's equal to 10^{100}. $(-10)^{101}$ is a very large negative number; if you raise a negative number to an odd number, the result is negative. $(-10)^{102}$ is a very large positive number, since the exponent is even. Of the answer choices, $(-10)^{101}$ has the least value.

28. **(D)** *Statistics: Arithmetic Mean*

You calculate the arithmetic mean of a numbers by dividing the sum of the numbers by a. The question says that A is the mean of three numbers—x, y, and z—so you should realize that option I, $A = \dfrac{x + y + z}{3}$, must be true. Try to manipulate this equation to see whether you can derive options II and III. If you multiply both sides of $A = \dfrac{x + y + z}{3}$ by 3, you get $3A = x + y + z$.

$$
\begin{aligned}
3A - x - y - z &= 0 \\
A + A + A - x - y - z &= 0 \\
(A - x) + (A - y) + (A - z) &= 0
\end{aligned}
$$

Option II must also be true, since it's a rewriting of the equation in option I. Option III says:

$$
\begin{aligned}
A + 3 &= \frac{x + y + z + 3}{3} \\
&= \frac{x + y + z}{3} + \frac{3}{3} \\
&= A + 1
\end{aligned}
$$

$$A + 3 \neq A + 1$$

Because you can't derive option III from option I, you know that option III is not necessarily true.

29. **(B)** *Functions: Evaluating Functions*

The phrasing of this question is the trickiest thing about it. The question says that $1 + x + \frac{x^2}{2} + \frac{x^3}{6}$ is an approximation of e^x. All this means is that the result of plugging x into $1 + x + \frac{x^2}{2} + \frac{x^3}{6}$ is close to the value of e^x. So to find e^1, simply plug $x = 1$ into $1 + x + \frac{x^2}{2} + \frac{x^3}{6}$:

$$e^1 \approx 1 + (1) + \frac{1^2}{2} + \frac{1^3}{6}$$
$$\approx 1 + 1 + \frac{1}{2} + \frac{1}{6}$$
$$\approx \frac{8}{3}$$

30. **(E)** *Trigonometry: Basic Functions*

If you look at the figure, you'll see that you have a right triangle $\triangle ACD$ with legs of lengths 7 and 8. You can use right triangle trig to find the angle $\angle CAD$. Since you're given the two legs of the triangle, you should use tangent to solve for the angle. Since 7 is opposite the angle and 8 is adjacent to it, you can write:

$$\tan \angle CAD = \frac{7}{8}$$
$$\angle CAD = \tan^{-1}\left(\frac{7}{8}\right)$$
$$\angle CAD \approx 41.2$$

31. **(A)** *Solid Geometry: Prisms*

The maximum distance between any two points in a cube is the long diagonal of the cube:

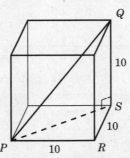

To find PQ, you first need to find PS. Since you know the sides of the cube are equal to 10, you can use the Pythagorean Theorem to find PS, which is the hypotenuse of the right triangle $\triangle PSR$:

$$(PS)^2 = 10^2 + 10^2$$
$$(PS)^2 = 200$$

You don't need to take the square root of 200 because you're now going to plug $(PS)^2$ into the Pythagorean Theorem to find PQ. In this case, PS and QS (a side of the cube) are the legs of a right triangle and PQ is its hypotenuse:

$$(PQ)^2 = 10^2 + (PS)^2$$
$$= 100 + 200$$
$$= 300$$
$$PQ = \sqrt{300}$$
$$\approx 17.3$$

32. (D) *Functions: Evaluating Functions; Coordinate Geometry: Lines and Slope*

Your first step should be to plug $(3 - x)$ into $f(x)$:

$$f(3 - x) = 6(3 - x) - 7$$
$$= 18 - 6x - 7$$
$$= -6x + 11$$

Now you have the line of an equation, $y = -6x + 11$. Since m is the slope of a line $y = mx + b$, the slope of the line in this question is –6.

33. (B) *Plane Geometry: Lines and Angles, Triangles*

Lines FB and AC must be parallel, since FB and DC are opposite sides of a rectangle. AB is a transversal line cutting the two parallel lines. When a transversal cuts parallel lines, the alternate interior angles created by these intersections are equal; in this case, $\angle EBF = \angle EAD$. You also know that $\angle EFB = \angle EDA = 90°$, since FD must be perpendicular to both FB and AD.

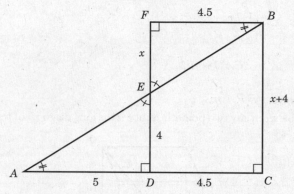

If two of the three angles in $\triangle AED$ and $\triangle BEF$ are equal, then their third angles must be equal as well. When the angles in two triangles are identical, the triangles are similar: $\triangle AED \sim \triangle BEF$. In other words, the proportions of the sides in the triangles are the same. You can set up a proportion to find the length of x:

$$\frac{EF}{FB} = \frac{ED}{DA}$$

$$\frac{x}{4.5} = \frac{4}{5}$$

$$x = \frac{18}{5}$$

$$x = 3.6$$

34. (C) *Trigonometry: Pythagorean Identities*

The Pythagorean trigonometric identities will help you solve tricky-looking trig problems on the Math IC. One of the most useful identities on the Math IC is: $\sin^2\theta + \cos^2\theta = 1$. Substitute this identity into the expression:

$$\left(\frac{2}{\sin^2\theta + \cos^2\theta - 4}\right)^2 = \left(\frac{2}{1 - 4}\right)^2$$

$$= \left(\frac{2}{-3}\right)^2$$

$$= \frac{4}{9}$$

35. **(E)** *Algebra: Polynomials*

For a quadratic equation $ax^2 + bx + c = 0$, the sum of the roots is equal to $-\frac{b}{a}$ and the product of the roots is equal to $\frac{c}{a}$. In $6x^2 - 18x + 7 = 0$, you have $a = 6$, $b = -18$, and $c = 7$. So the sum S of the roots is:

$$S = -\frac{b}{a}$$
$$= -\frac{(-18)}{6}$$
$$= 3$$

And the product P of the roots is:

$$P = \frac{c}{a}$$
$$= \frac{7}{6}$$

Now find the answer: $S - P = 3 - \frac{7}{6} = \frac{11}{6}$.

36. **(C)** *Plane Geometry: Polygons*

A rhombus is a parallelogram with sides of equal length. Draw a picture of the rhombus described in the question:

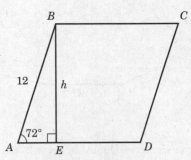

The area of a rhombus is its base multiplied by its height. You know that the base of the rhombus is 12, since all the sides have length 12, but you need to calculate the height. If you draw a perpendicular line down from point B, you'll create the right triangle, $\triangle ABE$, which has a hypotenuse 12. You can use simple trig to find the height:

$$\sin 72° = \frac{h}{12}$$
$$h = 12 \sin 72°$$

Now you can find the area of the rhombus:

$$A = bh$$
$$= 12 \cdot 12 \sin 72°$$
$$\approx 137$$

There's a faster way to answer this question. If you know that the area of a parallelogram is the product of the lengths of the sides multiplied by the sine of the included angle (the angle between the sides), you can jump straight away to:

$$A = 12 \cdot 12 \cdot \sin 72°$$
$$\approx 137$$

37. **(B)** *Algebra: Equation Solving, Exponential Growth and Decay*

Questions on exponential growth often show up on the Math IC, so you should make sure to memorize this formula: $A(t) = A_o(1 + r)^t$, where $A(t)$ is a value after time t; A_o is the initial value (when $t = 0$; r is the rate of inflation, written as a decimal; and t is time). In this case, $A_o = \$8.00$, $r = 0.06$, $t = 2003 - 1970 = 33$. Plug these values into the formula:

$$
\begin{aligned}
A(33) &= 8(1 + 0.06)^{33} \\
&= 8(1.06)^{33} \\
&\approx 54.72
\end{aligned}
$$

38. **(C)** *Functions: Transformations and Symmetry*

If $f(-x) = -f(x)$, the graph of $y = f(x)$ is said "symmetric with respect to the origin." (A good example of a function that's symmetric with respect to the origin is $f(x) = x^3$.) Of the graphs in the answer choices, only the one in choice (C) is symmetric with respect to the origin. Choices (A) and (D) are symmetric with respect to the y-axis, and choices (B) and (E) aren't symmetric at all.

39. **(A)** *Plane Geometry: Polygons*

You're looking for the smallest and largest possible values of AD that will allow $ABCD$ to remain a quadrilateral:

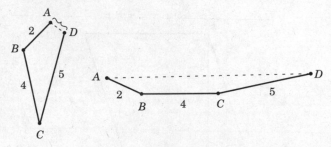

From the figure on the left, you can see that AD must be greater than zero in order for $ABCD$ to be a quadrilateral. If AD is equal to zero, A and D will be the same point and you'll have a triangle. From the figure on the right, you can see that AD must be less than the length of $AB + BC + CD$. If AD were equal to the sum of the three other lengths, you would have a line. You can put together the inequality:

$$
\begin{aligned}
0 &< AD < (AB + BC + CD) \\
0 &< AD < (2 + 4 + 5) \\
0 &< AD < 11
\end{aligned}
$$

40. **(D)** *Functions: Evaluating Functions*

You don't need to graph these equations in order to answer the problem. Factoring an equation will almost always simplify a problem on the Math IC. If you factor the numerator of $y_2 = \dfrac{x^2 - 4}{x - 2}$, you get

$$
\begin{aligned}
y_2 &= \frac{(x + 2)(x - 2)}{x - 2} \\
&= x + 2, \text{ as long as } x \neq 2
\end{aligned}
$$

You need to remember that x can't be equal to 2 here. If $x = 2$, y_2 is undefined because the denominator of the function is equal to zero. Since $y_1 = x + 2$, you know that $y_1 = y_2$, except when $x = 2$, where y_2 is undefined.

41. **(E)** *Plane Geometry: Polygons, Circles*

To find the area of the shaded region, you should subtract the area of the rectangle from the area of the circle. You can find the area of the rectangle by multiplying together its sides: $18 \cdot 24 = 432$. You need to find the radius of the circle in order to find its area. When you inscribe a rectangle in a circle, the diagonal of the rectangle is equal to the diameter of the circle, so the radius of the circle is equal to half the length of the rectangle's diagonal. Find the diagonal using the Pythagorean Theorem, where AC is the hypotenuse of a right triangle, and AB and BC are the triangle's sides:

$$(AC)^2 = 18^2 + 24^2$$
$$(AC)^2 = 900$$
$$AC = 30$$

The radius of the circle is $30 / 2 = 15$. Plug 15 into the formula for the area of a circle: $A = \pi r^2 = 225\pi$. Now find the area of the shaded region by the rectangle's area from the circle's:

$$\text{shaded region} = 225\pi - 432$$
$$\approx 274.9$$

42. **(A)** *Functions: Inverse Functions*

Solving an inverse function is a three-step process:
Step 1: Replace $f(x)$ with y.
Step 2: Switch x and y.
Step 3: Solve for y.
The expression you get for y is equal to $f^{-1}(x)$. Use these steps to find the inverse function of $f(x) = 3 - x^3$:

$$y = 3 - x^3$$
$$x = 3 - y^3$$
$$y^3 = 3 - x$$
$$y = \sqrt[3]{3 - x}$$
$$f^{-1}(x) = \sqrt[3]{3 - x}$$

The question asks you to evaluate $f^{-1}(x)$ at $x = 7$:

$$f^{-1}(7) = \sqrt[3]{3 - 7}$$
$$= \sqrt[3]{-4}$$
$$\approx -1.59$$

43. **(C)** *Functions: Compound Functions, Domain and Range*

First find the compound function $f(g(x))$ by plugging $g(x) = \sqrt{x}$ into $f(x) = x + 3$:

$$f(g(x)) = f(\sqrt{x})$$
$$= \sqrt{x} + 3$$

The range of this compound function is all the real values of $y = f(g(x))$. To find the range, you can use your calculator to graph the function. Alternatively, you can simply realize that $\sqrt{x}$ is always greater than or equal to zero (in order for it be a real number); thus $\sqrt{x} + 3$ must always be greater than or equal to 3.

44. **(B)** *Miscellaneous Math: Patterns*

The best way to solve this problem is to draw the fourth arrangement, continuing the pattern shown in the question:

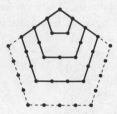

The fourth arrangement adds 13 new dots to the 22 dots in the third arrangement. The total number of dots in the fourth arrangement is 35.

45. **(D)** *Solid Geometry: Prisms; Algebra: Writing Equations*

The question asks you what happens to the volume of a cylinder when its height is halved and its radius doubled. First you need to know that the formula for the volume of a cylinder is $V = \pi r^2 h$; this equation gives you the volume of a cylinder with height h and radius r. To find out what happens when you halve the height and double the radius, plug in $\frac{h}{2}$ for the new height and $2r$ for the new radius. The volume of the altered cylinder is:

$$V' = \pi(2r)^2 \cdot \frac{h}{2}$$

$$= \pi(4r^2) \cdot \frac{h}{2}$$

$$= 2\pi r^2 h$$

The original cylinder's volume was $V = \pi r^2 h$. If $V' = 2\pi r^2 h$, then $V' = 2V$. In other words, the new volume, V', is double the old volume, V.

46. **(D)** *Functions: Evaluating Functions*

Since $x \Diamond y = \frac{x-y}{xy}$, solving $x \Diamond y \geq 0$ is the same as solving $\frac{x-y}{xy} \geq 0$. Split $\frac{x-y}{xy}$ into 2 fractions: $\frac{x}{xy} - \frac{y}{xy}$, which simplifies as $\frac{1}{y} - \frac{1}{x}$. Now set up the inequality:

$$\frac{1}{y} - \frac{1}{x} \geq 0$$

$$\frac{1}{y} \geq \frac{1}{x}$$

Now cross multiply (you don't need to worry about the direction of the inequality sign, since the question says x and y are both positive integers):

$$x \geq y$$

Since this inequality says that x is greater than or equal to y, both options I and III could be true.

47. **(E)** *Algebra: Writing Equations; Statistics: Probability*

You want the probability of choosing a black sock to be $\frac{7}{8}$, which means that 7 out of 8 socks in the bag are black. Make B equal to the number of black socks initially in the bag and T equal to the initial total of socks. The question tells you that B is equal to 160, and you can figure out that T is equal to 460, by adding 160 black sock and 300 red socks. Now have x equal the number of black socks you need to add to make the probability $\frac{7}{8}$. Remember that for every black sock you add, you increase not only the number of black socks but the total number of socks in the bag.

$$\frac{B+x}{T+x} = \frac{7}{8}$$

$$\frac{160+x}{460+x} = \frac{7}{8}$$

Cross multiply to get:

$$1280 + 8x = 3220 + 7x$$
$$x = 1940$$

48. **(E)** *Solid Geometry: Solids that Aren't Prisms*

This is a tricky question because there are two ways of illustrating the problem:

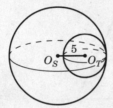 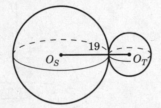

If the smaller sphere is inside the larger sphere, the distance between the origins is $12 - 7 = 5$. If the smaller sphere touches the outside of the larger sphere, the distance between the two origins is $12 + 7 = 19$. The question doesn't tell you whether it wants the smaller sphere to be inside or outside the larger sphere, so there isn't enough information to answer this question.

49. **(A)** *Solid Geometry: Prisms*

Draw a picture of a rectangular solid:

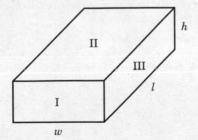

The question asks you for the volume of the rectangular solid. You know the following about the solid: the area of face I is equal to $w \cdot h$; the area of face II is equal to $w \cdot l$; the area of face III is equal to $l \cdot h$. The trick to getting this question is multiplying:

$$\begin{aligned}
(\text{face I}) \cdot (\text{face II}) \cdot (\text{face III}) &= (w \cdot h)(w \cdot l)(l \cdot h) \\
&= w^2 l^2 h^2 \\
&= (w \cdot l \cdot h)^2
\end{aligned}$$

Since the volume equals $w \cdot l \cdot h$, the volume squared equals $(w \cdot l \cdot h)^2$. To find the volume of this rectangular solid, multiply together the areas of the three faces and take the square root of this number.

$$\begin{aligned}
\text{Volume} &= \sqrt{(15) \cdot (7) \cdot (4.2)} \\
&= 21
\end{aligned}$$

50. **(B)** *Solid Geometry: Solids that Aren't Prisms*

The formula for the lateral surface area of a cone is given to you on the formula page at the beginning of the test. The formula is $S = \frac{1}{2}cl$, where c is the circumference of the base and l is the slant height. Draw a picture of the cone:

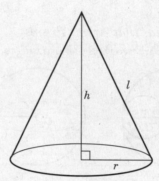

The radius r, the height h, and the slant height l of the cone form a right triangle, so you know $l^2 = r^2 + h^2$ and $l = \sqrt{r^2 + h^2}$. The circumference of the base is equal to $2\pi r$. Plug these two values into the lateral area formula, and you get $S = \frac{1}{2}(2\pi r)(\sqrt{r^2 + h^2})$, which reduces to $S = \pi r\sqrt{r^2 + h^2}$. The question also tells you that the lateral area of the cone is equal to twice the area of the base, which is πr^2, so you have $S = 2\pi r^2$. Set these two equations for the lateral area equal to each other:

$$\pi r\sqrt{r^2 + h^2} = 2\pi r^2$$

$$\sqrt{r^2 + h^2} = 2r$$

Square both sides of the equation:

$$r^2 + h^2 = 4r^2$$

$$h^2 = 3r^2$$

$$h = r\sqrt{3}$$

SAT II Math IC
Practice Test 4

MATH IC TEST 4 ANSWER SHEET

1. Ⓐ Ⓑ Ⓒ Ⓓ Ⓔ	18. Ⓐ Ⓑ Ⓒ Ⓓ Ⓔ	35. Ⓐ Ⓑ Ⓒ Ⓓ Ⓔ
2. Ⓐ Ⓑ Ⓒ Ⓓ Ⓔ	19. Ⓐ Ⓑ Ⓒ Ⓓ Ⓔ	36. Ⓐ Ⓑ Ⓒ Ⓓ Ⓔ
3. Ⓐ Ⓑ Ⓒ Ⓓ Ⓔ	20. Ⓐ Ⓑ Ⓒ Ⓓ Ⓔ	37. Ⓐ Ⓑ Ⓒ Ⓓ Ⓔ
4. Ⓐ Ⓑ Ⓒ Ⓓ Ⓔ	21. Ⓐ Ⓑ Ⓒ Ⓓ Ⓔ	38. Ⓐ Ⓑ Ⓒ Ⓓ Ⓔ
5. Ⓐ Ⓑ Ⓒ Ⓓ Ⓔ	22. Ⓐ Ⓑ Ⓒ Ⓓ Ⓔ	39. Ⓐ Ⓑ Ⓒ Ⓓ Ⓔ
6. Ⓐ Ⓑ Ⓒ Ⓓ Ⓔ	23. Ⓐ Ⓑ Ⓒ Ⓓ Ⓔ	40. Ⓐ Ⓑ Ⓒ Ⓓ Ⓔ
7. Ⓐ Ⓑ Ⓒ Ⓓ Ⓔ	24. Ⓐ Ⓑ Ⓒ Ⓓ Ⓔ	41. Ⓐ Ⓑ Ⓒ Ⓓ Ⓔ
8. Ⓐ Ⓑ Ⓒ Ⓓ Ⓔ	25. Ⓐ Ⓑ Ⓒ Ⓓ Ⓔ	42. Ⓐ Ⓑ Ⓒ Ⓓ Ⓔ
9. Ⓐ Ⓑ Ⓒ Ⓓ Ⓔ	26. Ⓐ Ⓑ Ⓒ Ⓓ Ⓔ	43. Ⓐ Ⓑ Ⓒ Ⓓ Ⓔ
10. Ⓐ Ⓑ Ⓒ Ⓓ Ⓔ	27. Ⓐ Ⓑ Ⓒ Ⓓ Ⓔ	44. Ⓐ Ⓑ Ⓒ Ⓓ Ⓔ
11. Ⓐ Ⓑ Ⓒ Ⓓ Ⓔ	28. Ⓐ Ⓑ Ⓒ Ⓓ Ⓔ	45. Ⓐ Ⓑ Ⓒ Ⓓ Ⓔ
12. Ⓐ Ⓑ Ⓒ Ⓓ Ⓔ	29. Ⓐ Ⓑ Ⓒ Ⓓ Ⓔ	46. Ⓐ Ⓑ Ⓒ Ⓓ Ⓔ
13. Ⓐ Ⓑ Ⓒ Ⓓ Ⓔ	30. Ⓐ Ⓑ Ⓒ Ⓓ Ⓔ	47. Ⓐ Ⓑ Ⓒ Ⓓ Ⓔ
14. Ⓐ Ⓑ Ⓒ Ⓓ Ⓔ	31. Ⓐ Ⓑ Ⓒ Ⓓ Ⓔ	48. Ⓐ Ⓑ Ⓒ Ⓓ Ⓔ
15. Ⓐ Ⓑ Ⓒ Ⓓ Ⓔ	32. Ⓐ Ⓑ Ⓒ Ⓓ Ⓔ	49. Ⓐ Ⓑ Ⓒ Ⓓ Ⓔ
16. Ⓐ Ⓑ Ⓒ Ⓓ Ⓔ	33. Ⓐ Ⓑ Ⓒ Ⓓ Ⓔ	50. Ⓐ Ⓑ Ⓒ Ⓓ Ⓔ
17. Ⓐ Ⓑ Ⓒ Ⓓ Ⓔ	34. Ⓐ Ⓑ Ⓒ Ⓓ Ⓔ	

REFERENCE INFORMATION

THE FOLLOWING INFORMATION IS FOR YOUR REFERENCE IN ANSWERING SOME OF THE QUESTIONS IN THIS TEST:

Volume of a right circular cone with radius r and height h: $V = \frac{1}{3}\pi r^2 h$

Lateral area of a right circular cone with circumference of the base c and slaight height ℓ: $S = \frac{1}{2}c\ell$

Volume of a sphere with radius r: $V = \frac{4}{3}\pi r^3$

Surface area of a sphere with radius r: $S = 4\pi r^2$

Volume of a pyramid with base area B and height h: $V = \frac{1}{3}Bh$

MATHEMATICS LEVEL IC TEST

For each of the following problems, decide which is the BEST of the choices given. If the exact numerical value is not one of the choices, select the choice that best approximates this value. Then fill in the corresponding oval on the answer sheet.

<u>Notes:</u> (1) A calculator will be necessary for answering some (but not all) of the questions in this test. For each question you will have to decide whether or not you should use a calcuator. The calculator you use must be at least a scientific calculator; programmable calculators and calculators that can display graphs are permitted.

(2) For some questions in this test you may need to decide whether your calculator should be in radian or degree mode.

(3) Figures that accompany problems in this test are intended to provide information useful in solving the problems. They are drawn as accurately as possible EXCEPT when it is stated in a specific problem that its figure is not drawn to scale. All figures lie in a plane unless otherwise indicated.

(4) Unless otherwise specified, the domain of any function f is assumed to be the set of all real numbers x for which $f(x)$ is a real number.

(5) Reference information that may be useful in answering the questions in this test can be found on the page preceding Question 1.

USE THIS SPACE FOR SCRATCHWORK.

1. The remainder when 251 is divided by 13 is equal to the remainder when which of the following numbers is divided by 6?

    (A) 24
    (B) 25
    (C) 26
    (D) 27
    (E) 28

2. If $g(x) = \sqrt{x^2 - x}$, then $g(3) =$

    (A) $\sqrt{7}$
    (B) $\sqrt{6}$
    (C) 3
    (D) 2
    (E) 1

GO ON TO THE NEXT PAGE

3. If a machine can produce b buttons in m minutes, then what is the machine's rate of button production per hour?

(A) $\dfrac{60b}{m}$

(B) $\dfrac{b}{60m}$

(C) $\dfrac{60m}{b}$

(D) $\dfrac{m}{60b}$

(E) $\dfrac{b}{m}$

4. If $x \neq 0$, then $\dfrac{2x^2 + 3x}{x} =$

(A) $2x^2 + 3x$
(B) $2x^2 + 3$
(C) $2x + 3$
(D) $2x$
(E) 5

5. If $bx^2 = bx$ and if $x = -1$, then

(A) $b = 1$
(B) $b = -1$
(C) $b = 2$
(D) $b = 0$
(E) b is any real number

6. If $(2x - 3)(ax + b) = 4x^2 - 2x - 6$ for all real x, then which of the following must be true?

(A) $a = 4$ and $b = 1$
(B) $a = 3$ and $b = 2$
(C) $a = 3$ and $b = -2$
(D) $a = 2$ and $b = 2$
(E) $a = 1$ and $b = 2$

7. What is the distance between the points $(-1, 2)$ and $(4, -6)$?

(A) 9.4
(B) 9.3
(C) 9.2
(D) 6.2
(E) 6.1

GO ON TO THE NEXT PAGE

USE THIS SPACE FOR SCRATCHWORK.

8. If $3^{x+1} + 3^{x+2} = 36$, then $x =$

    (A) 0
    (B) 1
    (C) 2.5
    (D) 3
    (E) 5

9. If $h(x) = 2x + 1$ and $g(x) = 3 - 4x$, then $g(h(4)) =$

    (A) –35
    (B) –34
    (C) –33
    (D) –25
    (E) 33

10. In Figure 1, what is z in terms of x and y ?

    (A) $180 - x + y$
    (B) $180 - 2x$
    (C) $y - x$
    (D) $x - y$
    (E) $x + y$

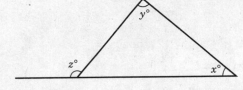

Figure 1

11. How many integer solutions does the equation
    $x(x - 2)(x - 4) - (x + 4)(x - 4)(x - 2) = 0$ have?

    (A) 4
    (B) 3
    (C) 2
    (D) 1
    (E) 0

12. If n is a positive odd integer, then which of the following <u>must</u> be
    a positive even integer?

    (A) $3n$

    (B) $3n + 1$

    (C) $3n + 2$

    (D) $\dfrac{3n + 1}{3}$

    (E) $3n + 4$

GO ON TO THE NEXT PAGE

13. If the cube root of a number is decreased by 4, the result is –1. What is the number?

    (A) 27
    (B) 24
    (C) –5
    (D) –27
    (E) –125

14. Which of the following lines is perpendicular to the line $y - 3 = 2(x - 5)$?

    (A) $y - 3 = \frac{1}{2}(x - 5)$

    (B) $y - 3 = -2(x + 5)$

    (C) $y + 3 = -(x - 5)$

    (D) $y + 3 = -\frac{1}{2}(x - 5)$

    (E) $y - 3 = -2(x - 5)$

15. If $(x + y)^2 = 12$, then $xy =$

    (A) $6 + \dfrac{x^2 + y^2}{2}$

    (B) $6 - \dfrac{x^2 + y^2}{2}$

    (C) $6 - \dfrac{x + y}{2}$

    (D) $\dfrac{12 - x + y}{2}$

    (E) $12 + x^2 + y^2$

16. If $g(x) = \sqrt{x^2 + 1}$, then what is the value of $g(2) + g(-2)$?

    (A) $\sqrt{5} + i$
    (B) 0
    (C) $\sqrt{8}$
    (D) $\sqrt{10}$
    (E) $2\sqrt{5}$

GO ON TO THE NEXT PAGE

USE THIS SPACE FOR SCRATCHWORK.

17. In Figure 2, what is the value of a?

   (A) 1.8
   (B) 2.4
   (C) 2.5
   (D) 2.6
   (E) 6.5

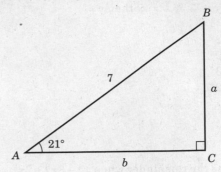

18. $\sqrt[3]{343x^9y^6z^3} =$

   (A) $49x^5y^3z^2$
   (B) $49x^6y^2z$
   (C) $7x^3y^2z$
   (D) $7x^3y^2z^2$
   (E) $7x^6y^3$

Note: Figure not drawn to scale.

Figure 2

19. $ab + 2i = 7 + bi$. If a and b are real numbers and if $i^2 = -1$, then what is the value of a?

   (A) 3.5
   (B) 4
   (C) 4.5
   (D) 5
   (E) $5 - i$

20. In Figure 3, if $\frac{x}{y} = 5$ then $y =$

    (A) 72°
    (B) 60°
    (C) 13°
    (D) 12°
    (E) 11°

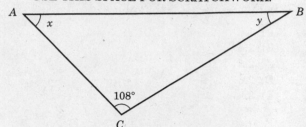

Note: Figure not drawn to scale.

Figure 3

21. What is the remainder when $x^4 + 3x^3 + 2x^2 + x + 5$ is divided by $x - 1$?

    (A) 13
    (B) 12
    (C) 11
    (D) 3
    (E) 0

22. If $0 < \theta < 90°$, then $(\sin^2\theta + \cos^2\theta + 3)^{1/2} =$

    (A) $\sqrt{1 - 2\sin\theta\cos\theta}$
    (B) $\sqrt{2\sin\theta\cos\theta}$
    (C) 0
    (D) 1
    (E) 2

23. John spends $12 on his daily commute to work and $15 a day on lunch. Pam spends $6 on her daily commute and $8 a day on lunch. If x is the average number of work days in a month, what is the difference between the expenditures of John and Pam?

    (A) $41
    (B) 41x$
    (C) 27x$
    (D) 13x$
    (E) $13

GO ON TO THE NEXT PAGE

24. Which of the following could be the graph of the <u>function</u> $y = f(x)$?

(A)
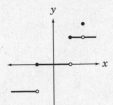

(B)
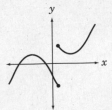

(C)
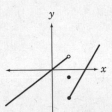

(D)
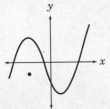

(E)
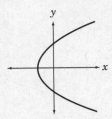

25. How many integers satisfy the inequality $|x - 5| \leq 3.5$?

(A) 5
(B) 6
(C) 7
(D) 8
(E) Infinitely many

26. If $x + y = 9$ and if $\dfrac{1}{x} + \dfrac{1}{y} = \dfrac{1}{2}$, then which of the following could be the value of x ?

(A) 7

(B) 6

(C) 5

(D) $\dfrac{1}{6}$

(E) $\dfrac{1}{3}$

GO ON TO THE NEXT PAGE

27. If $0 < \theta < 90°$, then $\dfrac{\tan\theta}{\sin\theta} - \dfrac{1}{\cos\theta} =$

    (A) -1
    (B) 0
    (C) 1
    (D) $\sin\theta - \cos\theta$
    (E) $\tan\theta - \sin\theta$

28. If an exterior angle in a triangle is equal in measure to its supplementary interior angle, then which of the following <u>must</u> be true of this triangle?

    (A) It is a scalene triangle.
    (B) It is an obtuse triangle.
    (C) It is an isosceles triangle.
    (D) It is an equilateral triangle.
    (E) It is a right triangle.

29. If the circumference of a circle is 5 times the value of the area of the circle, what is the radius of the circle?

    (A) 0.15
    (B) 0.18
    (C) 0.2
    (D) 0.4
    (E) 0.6

GO ON TO THE NEXT PAGE

30. Figure 4 shows two similar triangles: $\triangle ABC$ and $\triangle DEF$. If the area of $\triangle ABC$ is 4 times the area of $\triangle DEF$, what is the value of the length of side DF?

   (A) 14
   (B) 13
   (C) 12
   (D) 7
   (E) Not enough information to tell

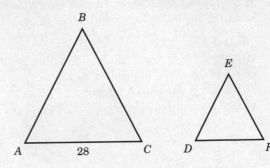

Note: Figure not drawn to scale.
Figure 4

31. If $f(x) = |x| - 3$ for $-3 \le x \le 4$, then the range of $f(x)$ is

   (A) $0 \le f(x) \le 1$
   (B) $-3 \le f(x) \le 0$
   (C) $-3 \le f(x) \le 1$
   (D) $-3 \le f(x) \le 2$
   (E) $-3 \le f(x) \le 3$

32. If $f(x) = \dfrac{x+1}{5}$ and if $g(x) = f^{-1}(x)$, then what is $g(3)$?

   (A) $\dfrac{4}{5}$

   (B) 10

   (C) 11

   (D) 13

   (E) 14

33. Sara's overall grade in a class is based entirely on her quiz and test scores. Quizzes count for 35% of her overall grade, and her quiz average is 72. What is her approximate test average if her overall average is 84?

   (A) 84.5
   (B) 90.1
   (C) 90.5
   (D) 91
   (E) 99

GO ON TO THE NEXT PAGE

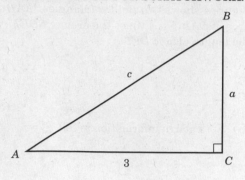

Figure 5

34. If the area of $\triangle ABC$ (shown in Figure 5) is an integer, then which of the following <u>must</u> be true of a?

    (A) $a = 2$
    (B) $a = 4$
    (C) a is a positive multiple of 4
    (D) a is a positive even integer
    (E) a is a positive integer

35. If line l is the perpendicular bisector of a line segment with endpoints $(1, 3)$ and $(5, 11)$, then what is the slope of the line l?

    (A) -2

    (B) $-\dfrac{1}{2}$

    (C) $\dfrac{1}{2}$

    (D) 2

    (E) 8

36. If y varies inversely with x, and if $y = 10$ when $x = 1.2$, then what is the value of x when $y = 30$?

    (A) 0.4
    (B) 0.6
    (C) 0.8
    (D) 10
    (E) 12

37. If the sides of a right triangle are in a ratio of $1 : 2 : c$ and if $c > 2$, then c must equal

    (A) $\sqrt{5}$
    (B) 3
    (C) 5
    (D) 6
    (E) $\sqrt{37}$

GO ON TO THE NEXT PAGE

38. If $\log_{16} 4 = x$, then x must equal

   (A) 4

   (B) 3

   (C) 2

   (D) 1

   (E) $\frac{1}{2}$

39. Line l intersects plane P perpendicularly at point p. Line m intersects line l perpendicularly at point q. If p and q are distinct, then which of the following must be true?

   (A) Line m is parallel to line l.
   (B) Line m intersects plane P at one point.
   (C) Line m is contained in plane P.
   (D) Line m is parallel to plane P.
   (E) Line m is perpendicular to plane P.

40. If $f(x) = \dfrac{1}{x^2 - 9}$ and if $h(x) = 3x$, then the domain of $f(h(x))$ is given by

   (A) All real numbers
   (B) All real numbers except $x = -3$ and $x = 3$
   (C) All real numbers except $x = -1$ and $x = 1$
   (D) All real numbers except $x = 1$
   (E) All real numbers except $x = 0$

GO ON TO THE NEXT PAGE

41. Which of the following is the graph of $y \le \sqrt{x}$ and $y \ge 1$?

(A)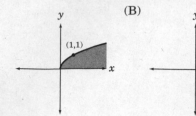

(B)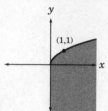

(C)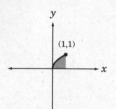

(D)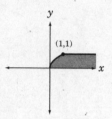

(E)

42. If $0 < \theta < 90°$ and if $\tan\theta = 7$, then $\cos(2\theta) =$

(A) 0.96
(B) 0.58
(C) 0.14
(D) −0.14
(E) −0.96

43. A cone and a sphere have equal volumes, and the radius of the cone's bottom equals the radius of the sphere. What is the height of the cone if the volume of the sphere is 972π ?

(A) 18
(B) 24
(C) 27
(D) 36
(E) 37

GO ON TO THE NEXT PAGE

44. If $f(x) = \dfrac{x+1}{3}$, what is $f(f^{-1}(f(5)))$?

    (A) -14
    (B) 0
    (C) 1
    (D) 2
    (E) 3

45. In Figure 6, a right circular cone is cut by a plane parallel to the base of the cone. If the radius and height of the cone have length 9, and if the distance from the plane to the cone's base is 6, what is the ratio of the volume of the part of the cone above the plane to the volume of the part of the cone below the plane?

    (A) $\dfrac{1}{27}$

    (B) $\dfrac{1}{26}$

    (C) $\dfrac{1}{3}$

    (D) $\dfrac{2}{3}$

    (E) $\dfrac{3}{11}$

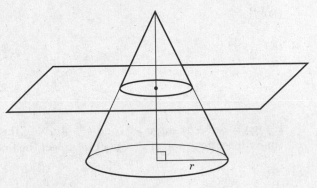

Figure 6

46. If $\dfrac{1}{x^2} < \dfrac{1}{y^2}$ and if $x \neq 0$ and $y \neq 0$, which of the following <u>could</u> be true?

    I. $x > y$
    II. $x < -y$
    III. $x > -y$

    (A) I only
    (B) II only
    (C) I and II only
    (D) I and III only
    (E) I, II, and III

47. If line segment AB and line segment CD bisect each other perpendicularly and if $AB = 12$ and $CD = 6$, then what is the measure of $\angle CAD$?

    (A) $26.57°$
    (B) $52.89°$
    (C) $53.13°$
    (D) $61.27°$
    (E) $63.05°$

GO ON TO THE NEXT PAGE

48. A box contains 5 marbles: 2 red and 3 yellow. If 3 marbles are picked from the box, what is the probability that <u>at least</u> one of them is red?

    (A) $\dfrac{9}{10}$

    (B) $\dfrac{4}{5}$

    (C) $\dfrac{7}{10}$

    (D) $\dfrac{3}{5}$

    (E) $\dfrac{1}{2}$

49. If $p(x) = ax^2 + bx + c$, $a > 0$, and $b^2 - 4ac < 0$, then how many times does the graph of $y = p(x)$ intersect the line $y = -1$?

    (A) 3
    (B) 2
    (C) 1
    (D) 0
    (E) Not enough information to tell

50. In Figure 7, chord AB is parallel to chord CD. If the length of chord AB is 16 and the length of chord CD is 12 and if the radius of the circle is 10, what is the distance between the chords?

    (A) 1
    (B) $\sqrt{2}$
    (C) 2
    (D) $2\sqrt{2}$
    (E) $2\sqrt{3}$

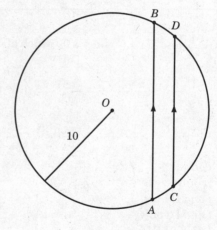

Figure 7

S T O P

IF YOU FINISH BEFORE TIME IS CALLED, YOU MAY CHECK YOUR WORK ON THIS TEST ONLY.
DO NOT TURN TO ANY OTHER TEST IN THIS BOOK.

SAT II Math IC
Practice Test 4
Explanations

Calculating Your Score

Question Number	Correct Answer	Right	Wrong	Question Number	Correct Answer	Right	Wrong	Question Number	Correct Answer	Right	Wrong
1.	E			18.	C			35.	B		
2.	B			19.	A			36.	A		
3.	A			20.	D			37.	A		
4.	C			21.	B			38.	E		
5.	D			22.	E			39.	D		
6.	D			23.	D			40.	C		
7.	A			24.	A			41.	B		
8.	B			25.	C			42.	E		
9.	C			26.	B			43.	D		
10.	E			27.	B			44.	D		
11.	C			28.	E			45.	B		
12.	B			29.	D			46.	E		
13.	A			30.	A			47.	C		
14.	D			31.	C			48.	A		
15.	B			32.	E			49.	D		
16.	E			33.	C			50.	C		
17.	C			34.	D						

Your raw score for the SAT II Math IC test is calculated from the number of questions you answer correctly and incorrectly. Once you have determined your composite score, use the conversion table on page 18 of this book to calculate your scaled score. To calculate your raw score, count the number of questions you answered correctly: _____
A

Count the number of questions you answered incorrectly, and multiply that number by $\frac{1}{4}$:

$$\underline{} \times \frac{1}{4} = \underline{}$$
B   C

Subtract the value in field C from value in field A: _____
D

Round the number in field D to the nearest whole number. This is your raw score: _____
E

Math IC Test 4 Explanations

1.   **(E)**   *Fundamentals: Integers*

First find the remainder when 251 is divided by 13: $\frac{251}{19} = 19 + \frac{4}{13}$, where 4 is the remainder. Now divide each of the answer choices by 6 to see which answer choice leaves a remainder of 4. Choice (E) produces the right remainder: $\frac{28}{6} = 4 + \frac{4}{6}$.

2.   **(B)**   *Functions: Evaluating Functions*

Find g(3) by plugging $x = 3$ into the function $g(x) = \sqrt{x^2 - x}$:

$$
\begin{aligned}
g(3) &= \sqrt{3^2 - 3} \\
&= \sqrt{9 - 3} \\
&= \sqrt{6}
\end{aligned}
$$

3.   **(A)**   *Algebra: Writing Equations, Word Problems*

The question says that the machine produces b buttons in m minutes. In other words, its rate of production is $\frac{b}{m}$, or b buttons per m minutes. Since you're asked to find the machine's rate of production per hour, you need to convert minutes to hours. There are 60 minutes in 1 hour, or $\frac{60 \text{ minutes}}{1 \text{ hour}}$. Multiply this expression by $\frac{b}{m}$, canceling out the minutes:

$$
\frac{b \text{ buttons}}{m \text{ minutes}} \times \frac{60 \text{ minutes}}{1 \text{ hour}} = \frac{60b \text{ buttons}}{m \text{ hour}}
$$

4.   **(C)**   *Algebra: Algebraic Manipulation*

All you need to do is simplify the expression given in the question.

$$
\frac{2x^2 + 3x}{x} = \frac{x(2x + 3)}{x}
$$

The x's cancel out of the numerator and denominator, leaving you with:

$$
= 2x + 3
$$

5.   **(D)**   *Fundamentals: Integers*

Plug $x = -1$ into $bx^2 = bx$:

$$
\begin{aligned}
b(-1)^2 &= -b \\
b &= -b
\end{aligned}
$$

If $b = -b$, then b must be equal to zero, since zero is the only number which is neither positive nor negative.

6.   **(D)**   *Algebra: Polynomials*

On the Math IC, multiplying out a factored polynomial will almost always reveal a solution to the problem. Multiply out $(2x - 3)(ax + b)$ using FOIL:

$$
\begin{aligned}
(2x - 3)(ax + b) &= 2ax^2 + 2bx - 3ax - 3b \\
&= 2ax^2 + (2b - 3a)x - 3b
\end{aligned}
$$

Now set this polynomial equal to $4x^2 - 2x - 6$:

$$2ax^2 + (2b - 3a)x - 3b = 4x^2 - 2x - 6$$

Since these polynomials are equal, you know that the corresponding x^2, x, and constant terms must also be equal. To find a, set the x^2 terms equal to each other:

$$2ax^2 = 4x^2$$
$$a = 2$$

Now find b by setting the constant terms equal to each other:

$$-3b = -6$$
$$b = 2$$

You can double check these values for a and b by plugging them into:

$$(2b - 3a)x = -2x$$
$$(2 \times 2 - 3 \times 2)x = -2x$$
$$-2x = -2x$$

7. (A) Coordinate Geometry: Lines and Distance

You definitely need to memorize the distance formula for the Math IC. The distance in a plane between the points (x_1, y_1) and (x_2, y_2) is given by the formula: $d = \sqrt{(x_1 - x_2)^2 + (y_1 - y_2)^2}$. Plug $(-1, 2)$ and $(4, -6)$ into this formula:

$$
\begin{aligned}
d &= \sqrt{(-1 - 4)^2 + (2 - (-6))^2} \\
&= \sqrt{(-5)^2 + 8^2} \\
&= \sqrt{89} \\
&= 9.4
\end{aligned}
$$

8. (B) Fundamentals: Exponents

The best way to answer this question is to use the law of exponents that says $a^{x+y} = a^x \cdot a^y$. Apply this law to the terms 3^{x+1} and 3^{x+2}:

$$3^{x+1} + 3^{x+2} = 3^x \cdot 3^1 + 3^x \cdot 3^2$$

Factor out 3^x:

$$
\begin{aligned}
3^x \cdot 3^1 + 3^x \cdot 3^2 &= 3^x(3 + 3^2) \\
&= 3^x(12)
\end{aligned}
$$

Now set this expression equal to 36:

$$
\begin{aligned}
3^x(12) &= 36 \\
3^x &= 3 \\
3^x &= 3^1 \\
x &= 1
\end{aligned}
$$

9. (C) Functions: Compound Functions

To solve the compound function $g(h(4))$, first evaluate $h(4)$ by plugging $x = 4$ into $h(x)$.

$$
\begin{aligned}
h(x) &= 2x + 1 \\
h(4) &= 2(4) + 1 \\
&= 9
\end{aligned}
$$

Now plug $x = 9$ into $g(x)$:

$$g(x) = 3 - 4x$$
$$g(9) = 3 - 4(9)$$
$$= 3 - 36$$
$$= -33$$

10. **(E)** *Plane Geometry: Triangles*

Take a look at the figure.

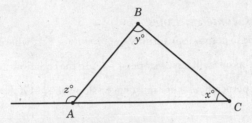

You can see that $z°$ and $\angle BAC$ are supplementary angles; in other words, $\angle BAC = 180° - z°$. You also know that the three angles in a triangle add up to $180°$, so in $\triangle ABC$, $x° + y° + (180° - z°) = 180°$. If you subtract $(180° - z°)$ from both sides of the equation, you end up with $x° + y° = z°$.

Another solution to this problem is to recognize that $z°$ is an exterior angle of $\triangle ABC$. An exterior angle of a triangle must equal the sum of the remote interior angles of the triangle; in other words, the exterior angle $z°$ must equal $x° + y°$.

11. **(C)** *Algebra: Polynomials*

Instead of multiplying out this equation, you should continue factoring. Both of the expressions on the left side of the equation share the factors $(x - 2)$ and $(x - 4)$.

$$x(x - 2)(x - 4) - (x + 4)(x - 2)(x - 4) = 0$$
$$(x - 2)(x - 4)[x - (x + 4)] = 0$$
$$(x - 2)(x - 4)(-4) = 0$$

This equation has two solutions: $x = 2$ and $x = 4$.

12. **(B)** *Fundamentals: Integers*

The easiest way to solve this problem is to choose a positive odd number for n and plug it into the answer choices. The correct answer choice will produce a positive even integer. Try plugging in $n = 1$. When you plug $n = 1$ into choice (B), you get:

$$3n + 1 = 3(1) + 1$$
$$= 4$$

Choice (B) is the only answer choice that produces a positive even integer. If you want to double check your answer, try plugging in another value for n, such as $n = 3$.

You can also solve the problem by remembering two rules of integers: one, the product of two odd numbers is another odd number; two, the sum of two odd numbers is an even number. In choice (B), the odd number 3 is multiplied by the odd number n, producing another odd number, $3n$. Then the odd number 1 is added to the odd number $3n$, producing an even number, $3n + 1$.

13. **(A)** *Algebra: Writing Equations*

You need to translate the question into an algebraic equation, making x the number you want to find. The cube root of x is $\sqrt[3]{x}$. If you decrease the cube root by 4, you get $\sqrt[3]{x} - 4$. The question tells you that this expression is equal to –1, so you have:

$$\sqrt[3]{x} - 4 = -1$$
$$\sqrt[3]{x} = 3$$
$$x = 3^3$$
$$= 27$$

14. **(D)** *Coordinate Geometry: Lines*

The question gives you a line in point-slope form: $y - y_1 = m(x - x_1)$, where m is the slope of the line. A line that's perpendicular to this one will have a slope of $-\dfrac{1}{m}$. In the equation $y - 3 = 2(x - 5)$, the slope m equals 2, so you know that a perpendicular line must have a slope of $-\dfrac{1}{2}$. Of the answer choices, only choice (D) has a slope of $-\dfrac{1}{2}$.

15. **(B)** *Algebra: Algebraic Manipulation*

When you see a factored polynomial like $(x + y)^2$, you should try multiplying it out.

$$(x + y)^2 = x^2 + 2xy + y^2$$

Now set this polynomial equal to 12:

$$x^2 + 2xy + y^2 = 12$$

$$2xy = 12 - (x^2 + y^2)$$

$$xy = \frac{12 - (x^2 + y^2)}{2}$$

$$= 6 - \frac{x^2 + y^2}{2}$$

16. **(E)** *Functions: Evaluating Functions*

First evaluate $g(x) = \sqrt{x^2 + 1}$ at $x = 2$ and at $x = -2$:

$$g(2) = \sqrt{2^2 + 1}$$
$$= \sqrt{5}$$
$$g(-2) = \sqrt{(-2)^2 + 1}$$
$$= \sqrt{5}$$

Now add $g(2)$ to $g(-2)$:

$$g(2) + g(-2) = \sqrt{5} + \sqrt{5}$$
$$= 2\sqrt{5}$$

17. **(C)** *Trigonometry: Basic Functions*

You're asked to find one of the legs of a right triangle based on the opposite angle and the hypotenuse.

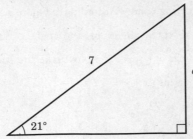

The easiest way to solve for the leg a is to use the sine of $21°$, since $\sin 21° = \dfrac{\text{opposite}}{\text{hypotenuse}}$. Plug the hypotenuse into this trig function, and find a:

$$\sin 21° = \frac{a}{7}$$
$$a = 7\sin 21°$$
$$= 2.5$$

18. **(C)** *Algebra: Algebraic Manipulation, Exponents*

You should use the law of exponents to solve this problem. Since $\sqrt[3]{x} = x^{1/3}$, you can rewrite $\sqrt[3]{343x^9y^6z^3}$ as:

$$\sqrt[3]{343x^9y^6z^3} = (343x^9y^6z^3)^{1/3}$$

Now distribute the exponent to each of the terms in the expression, using two rules of exponents—$(x \cdot y)^p = x^p \cdot y^p$ and $(x^n)^{1/p} = x^{n/p}$:

$$= 343^{1/3}(x^{9/3})(y^{6/3})(z^{3/3})$$
$$= 7x^3y^2z$$

19. **(A)** *Miscellaneous Math: Complex Numbers*

The solution to this problem doesn't really involve the imaginary number i. The question tells you that i is imaginary, so you know that you're dealing with complex numbers (numbers with imaginary and real components). The standard form of a complex number is $c + di$, where c and d are real numbers. In this question you have two complex numbers: $ab + 2i$ and $7 + bi$. Since these two complex numbers are equal, you know that their real terms are equal to each other and that their imaginary terms are equal to each other. First solve for b by equating the imaginary terms:

$$2i = bi$$
$$b = 2$$

Now solve for a by equating the real terms:

$$ab = 7$$
$$a(2) = 7$$
$$a = 3.5$$

20. **(D)** *Plane Geometry: Triangles; Algebra: Systems of Equations*

In this problem, you have two unknowns, x and y, and one equation, $\frac{x}{y} = 5$. In order to solve for y, you need to write another equation involving x and y. According to Figure 3, x and y are two angles in $\triangle ABC$, and $108°$ is the third. Since the three angles of a triangle add up to $180°$, you know that $x + y + 108° = 180°$, which becomes $x + y = 72°$. Now take the equation $\frac{x}{y} = 5$ and rewrite it as $x = 5y$. You can plug this value for x into $x + y = 72°$:

$$
\begin{aligned}
x + y &= 72° \\
5y + y &= 72° \\
6y &= 72° \\
y &= 12°
\end{aligned}
$$

21. **(B)** *Algebra: Polynomials*

You need to know polynomial long division for the Math IC. The polynomial version of long division says that any polynomial $P(x)$ can be written as $P(x) = (x - a) \cdot Q(x) + R$, where $(x - a)$ is the divisor, $Q(x)$ is the quotient, and R is the remainder. The remainder R can be found by plugging a into $P(x)$, since $P(a) = (a - a) \cdot Q(a) + R = R$. In this case, $P(x) = x^4 + 3x^3 + 2x^2 + x + 5$, and $a = 1$ since the divisor is $(x - 1)$. To find the remainder, plug 1 into $P(x)$:

$$
\begin{aligned}
P(1) &= 1^4 + 3 \cdot 1^3 + 2 \cdot 1^2 + 1 + 5 \\
&= 12
\end{aligned}
$$

22. **(E)** *Trigonometry: Pythagorean Identities*

Solving this problem is pretty easy if you can remember the the Pythagorean Trigonometric Identity $\sin^2\theta + \cos^2\theta = 1$:

$$
\begin{aligned}
(\sin^2\theta + \cos^2\theta + 3)^{1/2} &= (1 + 3)^{1/2} \\
&= (4)^{1/2} \\
&= \sqrt{4} \\
&= 2
\end{aligned}
$$

This identity will come in handy on the Math IC, so you should definitely memorize it before the test.

23. **(D)** *Algebra: Writing Equations, Word Problems*

If John spends \$12 on his commute and \$15 on his lunch, then his expenditure per day is \$12 + \$15 = \$27. Over x days, he spends \$27x. If Pam spends \$6 on her commute and \$8 on lunch, then her expenditure per day is \$6 + \$8 = \$14. Over x days, she spends \$14x. The difference between their expenditures over x days is \$27x − \$14x = \$13x.

24. **(A)** *Functions: Graphs of Functions*

The definition of a function says that each input x produces only one output $f(x)$. You can test whether a graph is a function by using the vertical line test: wherever you place it along the graph, a vertical line must pass through only one point on the graph. If the line passes through more than one point, the graph is not a function. Use the vertical line test on the graphs in the answer choices. Only choice (A) passes the test and is a function.

25. **(C)** *Algebra: Inequalities, Absolute Value*

An inequality with an absolute value on one side is actually two inequalities. $|x - 5| \leq 3.5$ can be divided into $x - 5 \leq 3.5$ and $x - 5 \geq -3.5$. Simplify these inequalities:

$$x - 5 \leq 3.5$$
$$x \leq 8.5$$

And:

$$x - 5 \geq -3.5$$
$$x \geq 1.5$$

You can combine these inequalities as $1.5 \leq x \leq 8.5$. The set of integers between 1.5 and 8.5 is $\{2, 3, 4, 5, 6, 7, 8\}$, so there are 7 integers that satisfy the solution set of $|x - 5| \leq 3.5$.

26. **(B)** *Algebra: Systems of Equations*

You should use the two equations to solve for the two unknowns, x and y. First rewrite the equation $\frac{1}{x} + \frac{1}{y} = \frac{1}{2}$ to get x and y out of the denominator. Start by multiplying the equation by xy:

$$xy\left(\frac{1}{x} + \frac{1}{y} = \frac{1}{2}\right)$$
$$y + x = \frac{xy}{2}$$

Since the question tells you that $x + y = 9$, you can substitute 9 into the equation above:

$$9 = \frac{xy}{2}$$
$$18 = xy$$
$$y = \frac{18}{x}$$

Now plug this value for y into $x + y = 9$:

$$x + \frac{18}{x} = 9$$

Multiply this equation by x to get:

$$x^2 + 18 = 9x$$
$$x^2 - 9x + 18 = 0$$
$$(x - 6)(x - 3) = 0$$

The solution to this equation is $x = 3$ or $x = 6$. Choice (B) is correct because it says that x could equal 6.

27. **(B)** *Trigonometry: Basic Functions*

In general, when you see a trigonometric expression on the Math IC, you should try to rewrite it in terms of sine and cosine. In this problem, replace $\tan\theta$ with $\frac{\sin\theta}{\cos\theta}$:

$$\frac{\tan\theta}{\sin\theta} - \cos\theta = \frac{\frac{\sin\theta}{\cos\theta}}{\sin\theta} - \frac{1}{\cos\theta}$$
$$= \frac{\sin\theta}{\cos\theta} \cdot \frac{1}{\sin\theta} - \frac{1}{\cos\theta}$$
$$= \frac{1}{\cos\theta} - \frac{1}{\cos\theta}$$
$$= 0$$

28. (E) *Plane Geometry: Triangles*

First draw a picture of the situation described in the question:

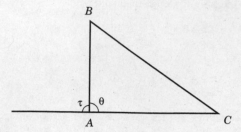

In this picture, τ is the exterior angle of the triangle, and θ is the supplementary interior angle. Supplementary angles equal $180°$, so $\tau + \theta = 180°$. Since the angles are equal to each other, they are each half of $180°$; in other words, they are $90°$ each. Since one of the angles in $\triangle ABC$ is $90°$, you know that $\triangle ABC$ is a right triangle and choice (E) must be true.

29. (D) *Plane Geometry: Circles*

The circumference of a circle with radius r is $C = 2\pi r$, and the area is $A = \pi r^2$. This problem states that a circle's circumference is five times the value of its area. You can translate this description into the equation $C = 5A$, or $2\pi r = 5\pi r^2$. Use this equation to solve for the radius of the circle:

$$2\pi r = 5\pi r^2$$
$$2r = 5r^2$$
$$2 = 5r$$
$$\frac{2}{5} = r$$
$$r = 0.4$$

30. (A) *Plane Geometry: Triangles*

Redraw the two triangles, including their heights:

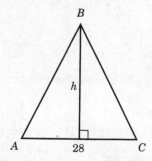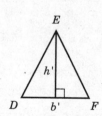

Since $\triangle ABC$ and $\triangle DEF$ are similar, all of their corresponding lengths (including their heights) are in a constant proportion. If you call this constant k, you can set up the following equations: $\frac{b^1}{28} = k$ and $\frac{h^1}{h} = k$. You can then rewrite these equations as $b^1 = 28k$ and $h^1 = hk$, respectively.

The formula for the area of a triangle is $\frac{1}{2}bh$, where b is the base and h is the height of the triangle. Using this formula, you can see that the area of $\triangle ABC = \frac{1}{2}(28)h$ and the area of $\triangle DEF = \frac{1}{2}b^1h^1$. Substitute the values for b^1 and h^1 into the area of $\triangle DEF$:

$$\text{Area}_{\triangle DEF} = \frac{1}{2}(28k)(hk)$$

$$= \frac{1}{2}(28h)k^2$$

Since the area of $\triangle ABC$ is four times as large as the area of $\triangle DEF$, you can set up the equation:

$$\text{Area}_{\triangle ABC} = 4 \times \text{Area}_{\triangle DEF}$$

$$\frac{1}{2}(28)h = 4\left[\frac{1}{2}(28h)k^2\right]$$

$$1 = 4k^2$$

$$k^2 = \frac{1}{4}$$

$$k = \frac{1}{2}$$

Now you can find DF, the base of $\triangle DEF$, by plugging $k = \frac{1}{2}$ into $b^1 = 28k$:

$$b^1 = 28\left(\frac{1}{2}\right)$$

$$= 14$$

31. **(C)** *Functions: Domain and Range*

The easiest way to find the range of $y = |x| - 3$ is to graph the equation on your calculator. If you set the calculator window to the domain $-3 \le x \le 4$, you can find the range by looking at the smallest and largest y-values in that domain. The graph should look like this:

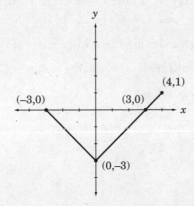

The range of y-values in this domain is $-3 \le y \le 1$.

32. **(E)** *Functions: Inverse Functions*

First find the inverse function of $f(x) = \dfrac{x+1}{5}$. There are three main steps in finding an inverse function. First, replace $f(x)$ with y:

$$y = \frac{x+1}{5}$$

Second, switch x and y:

$$x = \frac{y+1}{5}$$

Third, solve for y:

$$x = \frac{y+1}{5}$$

$$5x = y+1$$

$$5x - 1 = y$$

This equation is $g(x)$, the inverse function of $f(x)$. Find $g(3)$ by plugging $x = 3$ into $g(x)$:

$$g(3) = 5(3) - 1$$
$$= 14$$

33. **(C)** *Algebra: Writing Equations; Statistics: Arithmetic Mean*

You need to translate this problem into an algebraic expression. If the average of Sara's quizzes counts for 35% of her grade, then her test score average counts for 65% of her grade, since the overall score is based solely on tests and quizzes. Based on this information, you can write this equation: 0.35(quiz average) + 0.65(test average) = overall average. The question tells you that Sara's quiz average is 72 and her overall average is 84. If you plug these values into the equation above, you can find her test average, T.

$$0.35(72) + 0.65T = 84$$

$$0.65T = 84 - 0.35(72)$$

$$0.65T = 58.8$$

$$T = \frac{58.8}{0.65}$$

$$= 90.5$$

34. **(D)** *Fundamentals: Integers; Plane Geometry: Triangles*

The area of $\triangle ABC$ is equal to $\frac{1}{2}bh$, where b is the base and h is the height of the triangle. As you can see from Figure 5, the triangle's base is 3, and its height is a, so the area is $\frac{1}{2}(3)a$. The question says that the area is a positive *integer*, so you know that a needs to be a positive multiple of 2 (in other words, an even integer) in order to cancel the denominator out of $\frac{1}{2}(3)a$.

35. **(B)** *Coordinate Geometry: Lines*

All you need to know to answer this question is that l is perpendicular to the line segment. Since l and the line segment are perpendicular, the slope of l must be the negative reciprocal of the slope of the line segment. In other words, if the slope of the line segment is m, then the slope of l is $-\dfrac{1}{m}$. Find the slope between the points $(1, 3)$ and $(5, 11)$ by calculating the change in y over the change in x:

$$m = \frac{\Delta y}{\Delta x}$$

$$m = \frac{11 - 3}{5 - 1}$$

$$= \frac{8}{4}$$

$$= 2$$

If the slope of the line segment is 2, then the slope of l is the negative reciprocal of 2: $-\dfrac{1}{2}$.

36. **(A)** *Algebra: Writing Equations, Variation*

The question tells you that y varies inversely with x, which means that as y gets larger, x gets smaller in a constant proportion. You can write an equation to show this relationship: $y = \dfrac{k}{x}$, where k is the constant of variation. The question says that $y = 10$ when $x = 1.2$. You can plug these values into $y = \dfrac{k}{x}$ to find the constant k:

$$10 = \frac{k}{1.2}$$

$$k = 12$$

Now that you know k, you can figure out the value of x when $y = 30$:

$$30 = \frac{12}{x}$$

$$x = \frac{12}{30}$$

$$= \frac{2}{5}$$

$$= 0.4$$

37. **(A)** *Plane Geometry: Triangles*

The question says that the sides of a right triangle are in a ratio of $1:2:c$ and that $c > 2$, which means that c is the longest side (the hypotenuse) of the triangle. For the sake of simplicity, you can say that the lengths of the triangle *are* 1, 2, and c. Plug these lengths into the Pythagorean Theorem to solve for c:

$$1^2 + 2^2 = c^2$$
$$1 + 4 = c^2$$
$$5 = c^2$$
$$c = \sqrt{5}$$

38. **(E)** *Algebra: Equation Solving, Logarithms*

According to the definition of a logarithm, $\log_b a = x$ is equivalent to $b^x = a$. You can solve for x by applying this definition to the logarithm given in the question:

$$\log_{16} 4 = x$$
$$16^x = 4$$
$$(4^2)^x = 4^1$$
$$4^{2x} = 4^1$$

Since the bases of these terms are equal, the exponents must also be equal:

$$2x = 1$$
$$x = \frac{1}{2}$$

39. **(D)** *Plane Geometry: Lines and Planes*

Try drawing a picture of the situation described in the question:

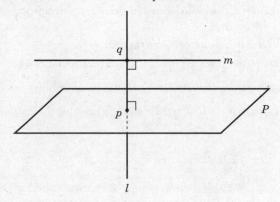

You should be able to see from this picture that the line m must run parallel to the plane P.

40. **(C)** *Functions: Compound Functions, Domain and Range*

First determine the compound function $f(h(x))$ by plugging $x = h(x)$ into $f(x) = \frac{1}{x^2 - 9}$. Since $h(x) = 3x$, you're looking for $f(3x)$:

$$f(h(x)) = f(3x)$$
$$= \frac{1}{(3x)^2 - 9}$$
$$= \frac{1}{9x^2 - 9}$$
$$= \frac{1}{9(x^2 - 1)}$$
$$= \frac{1}{9(x + 1)(x - 1)}$$

The domain of $f(x)$ contains all values of x that produce real values of $f(x)$. When solving for the domain of a function, you want to exclude values of x that make $f(x)$ undefined: for example, values of x that make the denominator of $f(x)$ equal to zero. In the domain of $f(h(x))$, $x \neq 1$ and $x \neq -1$, since those values make the denominator of the function equal zero.

41. **(B)** *Functions: Graphs of Functions*

The graph of the inequalities $y \le \sqrt{x}$ and $y \ge 1$ is the area of their intersection. The best way to answer this problem is to graph each of these inequalities and see how they intersect. The graph of $y \le \sqrt{x}$ is the set of all points below and including the curve $y = \sqrt{x}$:

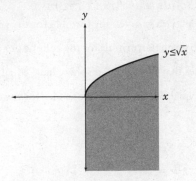

The graph of $y \ge 1$ is the set of all points above and including the line $y = 1$:

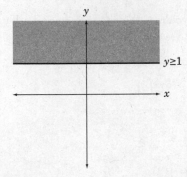

The intersection of these two graphs looks like this:

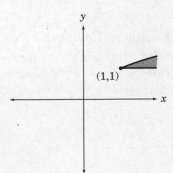

This graph is identical to the one shown in choice (B), the correct answer.

42. **(E)** *Trigonometry: Inverse Trigonometric Functions*

The question tells you that $\tan\theta = 7$ and asks you to find $\cos(2\theta)$. First, find θ by taking the inverse tangent of 7 on your calculator:

$$\theta = \tan^{-1}(7)$$
$$= 81.87°$$

Multiply θ by 2:

$$2\theta = 163.74°$$

Now you can find $\cos(2\theta)$:

$$\cos(2\theta) = \cos 163.74°$$
$$= -0.96$$

43. (D) *Solid Geometry: Solids that Aren't Prisms*

At the beginning of the test booklet, you're given the formula for the volume of a cone with radius r and height h: $v_c = \frac{1}{3}\pi r^2 h$. You're also given the formula for the volume of a sphere: $v_s = \frac{4}{3}\pi r^3$, where r is the sphere's radius. The question states that the cone and sphere have equal volumes and that the radii of the cone's base and of the sphere are equal. Set the volume formulas for the cone and the sphere equal to each other and solve for h:

$$v_c = v_s$$
$$\frac{1}{3}\pi r^2 h = \frac{4}{3}\pi r^3$$
$$h = 4r$$

You now have h in terms of r, but you're looking for a numerical value for h. Since the question also tells you that the sphere's volume is 972π, you can solve for r:

$$\frac{4}{3}\pi r^3 = 972\pi$$
$$r^3 = 972\left(\frac{3}{4}\right)$$
$$r^3 = 729$$
$$r = 9$$

Plug $r = 9$ into $h = 4r$:

$$h = 4(9)$$
$$= 36$$

44. (D) *Functions: Inverse Functions, Compound Functions*

You could solve this problem by finding $f^{-1}(x)$ and solving the compound function $f(f^{-1}(f(x)))$, but you'd waste a lot of time. The easiest (and fastest) way to find the answer is to realize that $f^{-1}(f(x)) = x$ for any x in the domains of both functions. According to this rule, $f(f^{-1}(f(5))) = f(5)$ since $f^{-1}(f(5)) = 5$. Evaluate $f(5)$:

$$f(x) = \frac{x+1}{3}$$
$$f(5) = \frac{5+1}{3}$$
$$= 2$$

45. **(B)** *Solid Geometry: Solids that Aren't Prisms*

One way to answer this problem is to find the volumes of the large and small cones. The formula for the volume of a cone (provided at the beginning of the test) involves the cone's height and radius, so you need to find these values for the small cone (the height and radius of the big cone are given in the question). The height of the small cone is the difference between the large cone's height and the distance between the large cone's base and the plane. Since the large cone's height is 9, and the distance between the base and the plane is 6, you know that the height of the small cone is 3. To help you find the small cone's radius, draw a picture of the problem:

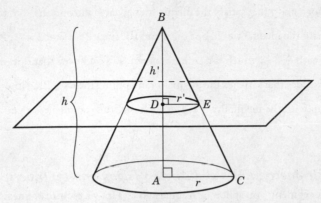

In the picture, you can see two similar triangles—$\triangle ABC$ and $\triangle DBE$—created by the heights, lateral heights, and radii of the two cones. You know these triangles are similar because their angles are the same. They both include a right angle and $\angle B$; since the angles of all triangles add up to $180°$, their third angles must also be equal. In similar triangles, the ratio of the triangles' sides is constant. You can set up a ratio to find r_1, using $r = 9$, $h = 9$, and $h_1 = 3$. Plug these values into the ratio $\frac{r}{h} = \frac{r_1}{h_1}$:

$$\frac{9}{9} = \frac{r_1}{3}$$

$$r_1 = 3$$

Now that you have the radius and height of the small cone, you can find the cone's volume:

$$V_{\text{small}} = \frac{1}{3}\pi(r_1)^2 h_1$$

$$= \frac{1}{3}\pi(3)^2(3)$$

$$= 9\pi$$

Now find the volume of the large cone:

$$V_{\text{large}} = \frac{1}{3}\pi(r)^2 h$$

$$= \frac{1}{3}\pi(9)^2(9)$$

$$= 243\pi$$

Find the volume of the part of the large cone beneath the plane by subtracting the volume of the small cone from the volume of the large cone:

$$V_{\text{bottom}} = 243\pi - 9\pi$$

$$= 234\pi$$

Finally, find the ratio of the small cone to the volume of the part of the large cone beneath the plane:

$$\frac{V_{small}}{V_{bottom}} = \frac{9\pi}{234\pi}$$

$$= \frac{1}{26}$$

46. **(E)** *Basic Math: Inequalities*

Since this problem asks you what *could* be true, rather than what *must* be true, you can solve it by plugging in different numbers for x and y that satisfy the inequalities given in the options. Try, for example, $x = 2$ and $y = 1$; these values satisfy the inequalities in options I and III, since $2 > 1$ and $2 > -1$. Plug these values into $\frac{1}{x^2} < \frac{1}{y^2}$. You end up with $\frac{1}{4} < \frac{1}{2}$, which is a true statement, so you know that options I and III could be true. Now try a set of values that satisfies the inequality in option II: $x < -y$. Plug in $x = -2$ and $y = -1$, since $-2 < -(-1)$. You end up with the inequality $\frac{1}{4} < 1$, which is a true statement, so you know that option II could also be true.

47. **(C)** *Plane Geometry: Lines and Angles; Trigonometry: Inverse Trigonometry*

When you bisect a line segment, you split it into equal halves. Draw a picture of lines AB and CD bisecting each other and connect the endpoints like this:

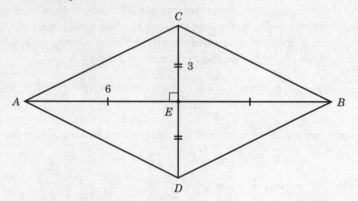

You should be able to tell from this drawing that $\angle CAD = 2\angle CAE$. You can find $\angle CAE$ using right triangle trig since you know the lengths of the two legs of $\triangle CAE : AE = 6$ and $CE = 3$.

$$\tan \angle CAE = \frac{3}{6}$$

To find $\angle CAE$, take the inverse tangent of both sides of the equation:

$$\angle CAE = \tan^{-1}\left(\frac{3}{6}\right)$$

$$= 26.565°$$

To find $\angle CAB$, multiply $\angle CAE$ by 2: $\angle CAB = 2\angle CAE = 53.13°$.

48. **(A)** *Statistics: Probability*

The question asks you for the probability of picking *at least one* red marble from the box. Since there are two red marbles total, you're solving for the probability of picking either one or two red marbles in your three picks. You can calculate the probability of picking *at least one* thing by subtracting the probability of picking none of those things from 1: $P(\text{at least one}) = 1 - P(\text{none})$. The probability of picking no red marbles is the same as the probability of picking all yellow marbles. The probability of picking a yellow marble out of the box for your first pick is $\frac{3}{5}$, since there are three yellow marbles and five marbles total. After the first pick, there are only two yellow marbles and four marbles total left in the box, so the probability that your second pick will be yellow is $\frac{2}{4}$. Finally, the probability that your third pick will be yellow is $\frac{1}{3}$, since the box now contains one yellow marble and three marbles total. Multiply these probabilities together to find the probability of picking no red marbles:

$$\begin{aligned} P(\text{none}) &= \frac{3}{5} \times \frac{2}{4} \times \frac{1}{3} \\ &= \frac{1}{10} \end{aligned}$$

Now subtract $P(\text{none})$ from 1 to find the probability of picking at least one red marble:

$$\begin{aligned} P(\text{at least one}) &= 1 - P(\text{none}) \\ &= 1 - \frac{1}{10} \\ &= \frac{9}{10} \end{aligned}$$

49. **(D)** *Functions: Graphs of Functions, Roots*

$p(x) = ax^2 + bx + c$ is a standard quadratic (U-shaped) polynomial. The question tells you that a, the coefficient of the x^2 term, is a positive number, so you know that the graph of the function opens upward. $b^2 - 4ac$ is called the discriminant of the function, and it's found using the coefficients of the polynomial. A function's discriminant tells you what kind of roots the polynomial has. If $b^2 - 4ac < 0$, then the polynomial has no real roots. If $b^2 - 4ac = 0$, then the function has one double root. If $b^2 - 4ac > 0$, then the function has two real roots. The function in this question has a discriminant that is less than zero, so it has no real roots, which means that it never crosses the x-axis. Since the graph opens upward and never crosses the x-axis, you know that the graph can't have any negative y-values; therefore, the graph of $p(x)$ never intersects the line $y = -1$, which is below the x-axis.

50. **(C)** *Plane Geometry: Circles*

You can create two isosceles triangles by connecting radii to points A, B, C, and D.

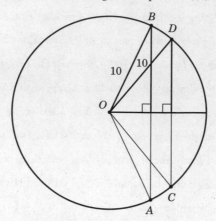

As you can see from this picture, the distance between the two chords is equal to the difference between the triangles' heights. You can find the triangles' heights using the Pythagorean Theorem:

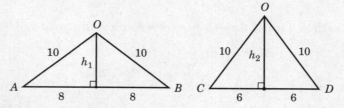

$\triangle OEB$ is a right triangle with a hypotenuse of 10 and legs of 8 and h_1. $\triangle OFD$ is a right triangle with a hypotenuse of 10 and legs of 6 and h_2. Plug these lengths into the Pythagorean Theorem, and solve for h_1 and h_2.

$$10^2 = 8^2 + (h_1)^2$$
$$(h_1)^2 = 36$$
$$h_1 = 6$$

And:

$$10^2 = 6^2 + (h_2)^2$$
$$(h_2)^2 = 64$$
$$h_2 = 8$$

The distance between the chords is given by $h_2 - h_1 = 8 - 6 = 2$.

SAT II Math IC
Practice Test 5

MATH IC TEST 5 ANSWER SHEET

1. Ⓐ Ⓑ Ⓒ Ⓓ Ⓔ	18. Ⓐ Ⓑ Ⓒ Ⓓ Ⓔ	35. Ⓐ Ⓑ Ⓒ Ⓓ Ⓔ
2. Ⓐ Ⓑ Ⓒ Ⓓ Ⓔ	19. Ⓐ Ⓑ Ⓒ Ⓓ Ⓔ	36. Ⓐ Ⓑ Ⓒ Ⓓ Ⓔ
3. Ⓐ Ⓑ Ⓒ Ⓓ Ⓔ	20. Ⓐ Ⓑ Ⓒ Ⓓ Ⓔ	37. Ⓐ Ⓑ Ⓒ Ⓓ Ⓔ
4. Ⓐ Ⓑ Ⓒ Ⓓ Ⓔ	21. Ⓐ Ⓑ Ⓒ Ⓓ Ⓔ	38. Ⓐ Ⓑ Ⓒ Ⓓ Ⓔ
5. Ⓐ Ⓑ Ⓒ Ⓓ Ⓔ	22. Ⓐ Ⓑ Ⓒ Ⓓ Ⓔ	39. Ⓐ Ⓑ Ⓒ Ⓓ Ⓔ
6. Ⓐ Ⓑ Ⓒ Ⓓ Ⓔ	23. Ⓐ Ⓑ Ⓒ Ⓓ Ⓔ	40. Ⓐ Ⓑ Ⓒ Ⓓ Ⓔ
7. Ⓐ Ⓑ Ⓒ Ⓓ Ⓔ	24. Ⓐ Ⓑ Ⓒ Ⓓ Ⓔ	41. Ⓐ Ⓑ Ⓒ Ⓓ Ⓔ
8. Ⓐ Ⓑ Ⓒ Ⓓ Ⓔ	25. Ⓐ Ⓑ Ⓒ Ⓓ Ⓔ	42. Ⓐ Ⓑ Ⓒ Ⓓ Ⓔ
9. Ⓐ Ⓑ Ⓒ Ⓓ Ⓔ	26. Ⓐ Ⓑ Ⓒ Ⓓ Ⓔ	43. Ⓐ Ⓑ Ⓒ Ⓓ Ⓔ
10. Ⓐ Ⓑ Ⓒ Ⓓ Ⓔ	27. Ⓐ Ⓑ Ⓒ Ⓓ Ⓔ	44. Ⓐ Ⓑ Ⓒ Ⓓ Ⓔ
11. Ⓐ Ⓑ Ⓒ Ⓓ Ⓔ	28. Ⓐ Ⓑ Ⓒ Ⓓ Ⓔ	45. Ⓐ Ⓑ Ⓒ Ⓓ Ⓔ
12. Ⓐ Ⓑ Ⓒ Ⓓ Ⓔ	29. Ⓐ Ⓑ Ⓒ Ⓓ Ⓔ	46. Ⓐ Ⓑ Ⓒ Ⓓ Ⓔ
13. Ⓐ Ⓑ Ⓒ Ⓓ Ⓔ	30. Ⓐ Ⓑ Ⓒ Ⓓ Ⓔ	47. Ⓐ Ⓑ Ⓒ Ⓓ Ⓔ
14. Ⓐ Ⓑ Ⓒ Ⓓ Ⓔ	31. Ⓐ Ⓑ Ⓒ Ⓓ Ⓔ	48. Ⓐ Ⓑ Ⓒ Ⓓ Ⓔ
15. Ⓐ Ⓑ Ⓒ Ⓓ Ⓔ	32. Ⓐ Ⓑ Ⓒ Ⓓ Ⓔ	49. Ⓐ Ⓑ Ⓒ Ⓓ Ⓔ
16. Ⓐ Ⓑ Ⓒ Ⓓ Ⓔ	33. Ⓐ Ⓑ Ⓒ Ⓓ Ⓔ	50. Ⓐ Ⓑ Ⓒ Ⓓ Ⓔ
17. Ⓐ Ⓑ Ⓒ Ⓓ Ⓔ	34. Ⓐ Ⓑ Ⓒ Ⓓ Ⓔ	

REFERENCE INFORMATION

THE FOLLOWING INFORMATION IS FOR YOUR REFERENCE IN ANSWERING SOME OF THE QUESTIONS IN THIS TEST:

Volume of a right circular cone with radius r and height h: $V = \frac{1}{3}\pi r^2 h$

Lateral area of a right circular cone with circumference of the base c and slaight height ℓ: $S = \frac{1}{2}c\ell$

Volume of a sphere with radius r: $V = \frac{4}{3}\pi r^3$

Surface area of a sphere with radius r: $S = 4\pi r^2$

Volume of a pyramid with base area B and height h: $V = \frac{1}{3}Bh$

MATHEMATICS LEVEL IC TEST

For each of the following problems, decide which is the BEST of the choices given. If the exact numerical value is not one of the choices, select the choice that best approximates this value. Then fill in the corresponding oval on the answer sheet.

<u>Notes:</u> (1) A calculator will be necessary for answering some (but not all) of the questions in this test. For each question you will have to decide whether or not you should use a calcuator. The calculator you use must be at least a scientific calculator; programmable calculators and calculators that can display graphs are permitted.

(2) For some questions in this test you may need to decide whether your calculator should be in radian or degree mode.

(3) Figures that accompany problems in this test are intended to provide information useful in solving the problems. They are drawn as accurately as possible EXCEPT when it is stated in a specific problem that its figure is not drawn to scale. All figures lie in a plane unless otherwise indicated.

(4) Unless otherwise specified, the domain of any function f is assumed to be the set of all real numbers x for which $f(x)$ is a real number.

(5) Reference information that may be useful in answering the questions in this test can be found on the page preceding Question 1.

USE THIS SPACE FOR SCRATCHWORK.

1. If the area of a triangle is $18x^2$, and if its base and height are equal, what is the length of the base of the triangle?

    (A) 9
    (B) 3
    (C) x
    (D) $3x$
    (E) $6x$

2. Which of the following integers is <u>not</u> divisible by 2, 3, and 7?

    (A) 42
    (B) 96
    (C) 138
    (D) 398
    (E) 420

3. At what value of x do the lines $y = x + 1$ and $y = 1 - x$ intersect?

    (A) −1
    (B) 0
    (C) 1
    (D) 2
    (E) 3.5

GO ON TO THE NEXT PAGE

USE THIS SPACE FOR SCRATCHWORK.

4. If $\frac{2}{3x-1} = \frac{1}{13}$, then $x =$

(A) 9
(B) 3
(C) 1
(D) –2
(E) –3

5. In Figure 1, if $AC = x + 2$ and $BD = 12 - x$ and $BC = 3$, then what is the length of AD?

(A) 19
(B) 15
(C) 11
(D) $2x - 5$
(E) $2x + 13$

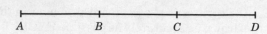

Figure 1

6. If $x = y^2$ and $y = \frac{z}{3}$, what is the value of x when $z = 9$?

(A) 1
(B) 3
(C) 8
(D) 9
(E) 36

GO ON TO THE NEXT PAGE

7. In Figure 2, what is the slope of segment AB?

    (A) $\dfrac{3}{2}$

    (B) $\dfrac{2}{3}$

    (C) $\dfrac{1}{2}$

    (D) $\dfrac{1}{3}$

    (E) $\dfrac{1}{4}$

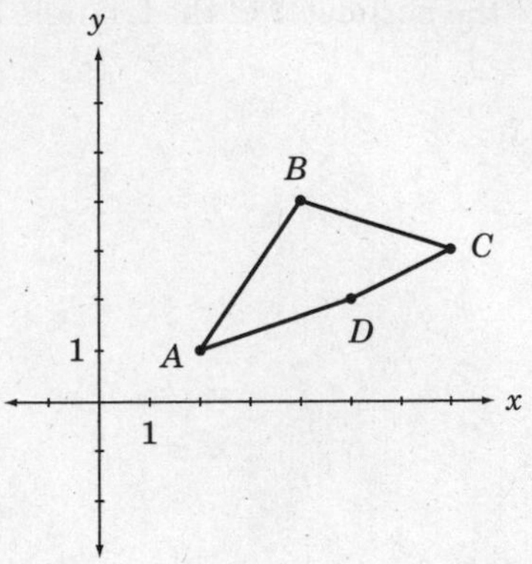

Figure 2

8. If $x \neq -3$, $\dfrac{x^2 + x - 6}{x + 3} =$

    (A) $x - 3$
    (B) $x + 2$
    (C) $x - 2$
    (D) 1
    (E) 2

9. If a recipe for two servings calls for x cups of flour, then how many quarts of flour will be required for 7 servings (1 quart = 4 cups)?

    (A) $\dfrac{8x}{7}$

    (B) $\dfrac{7x}{8}$

    (C) $\dfrac{7x}{4}$

    (D) $\dfrac{7x}{2}$

    (E) $3x$

10. What is the distance between the points $(-3, -7)$ and $(4, 16)$?

    (A) 12.36
    (B) 15.43
    (C) 18.77
    (D) 20.12
    (E) 24.04

GO ON TO THE NEXT PAGE

11. What is the perimeter of the triangle in Figure 3?

   (A) 27
   (B) 28.5
   (C) 47
   (D) 50
   (E) 58

USE THIS SPACE FOR SCRATCHWORK.

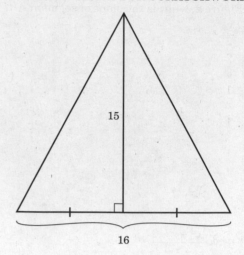

Figure 3

12. In Figure 4, what is the cosine of $\angle DAB$?

   (A) 0.50
   (B) 0.57
   (C) 0.61
   (D) 0.66
   (E) 0.83

13. If $3n + 7m = 27$ and n and m are both positive integers, then which of the following could be $n + m$?

   (A) 2
   (B) 3
   (C) 4
   (D) 5
   (E) 6

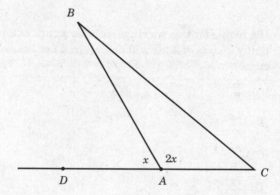

Figure 4

GO ON TO THE NEXT PAGE

USE THIS SPACE FOR SCRATCHWORK.

14. If $\dfrac{1}{t} + \dfrac{2}{3t} = \dfrac{1}{3}$, then $t =$

   (A) 6
   (B) 5
   (C) 4.5
   (D) 3.5
   (E) 2.5

15. In Figure 5, what is θ in terms of x and y?

   (A) $90 - x - y$
   (B) $90 - x + y$
   (C) $90 + x - y$
   (D) $180 - x - y$
   (E) $180 - x + y$

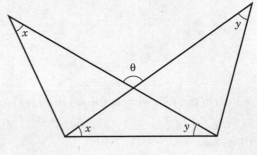

Figure 5

16. John can paint a house in d days. If John works for x days and then stops, then what fraction of the house remains unpainted in terms of x and d? (Assume $d > x$.)

   (A) $\dfrac{d - x}{d}$

   (B) $1 - \dfrac{d}{x}$

   (C) $\dfrac{x - d}{x}$

   (D) x

   (E) $d - x$

17. A line passes through the points $(k, k + 1)$ and $(2k, 2 - k)$. If the slope of the line is $\dfrac{1}{3}$, then what is the value of k?

   (A) $\dfrac{1}{7}$

   (B) $\dfrac{1}{3}$

   (C) $\dfrac{3}{7}$

   (D) $\dfrac{9}{4}$

   (E) $\dfrac{7}{3}$

GO ON TO THE NEXT PAGE ➤

18. If a positive integer is selected at random and then divided by 5, what is the probability that the remainder is even?

    (A) $\frac{1}{5}$

    (B) $\frac{2}{5}$

    (C) $\frac{3}{5}$

    (D) $\frac{4}{5}$

    (E) $\frac{5}{6}$

19. Which of the following is the solution set to $|x - 1| + 3 \leq 0$?

    (A) $-2 < x < 4$
    (B) $-2 \leq x \leq 4$
    (C) $x \leq -2$ or $x \geq 4$
    (D) $0 \leq x \leq 4$
    (E) The inequality has no solutions.

20. Let $x \otimes y$ be defined on all positive real numbers as
    $x \otimes y = \frac{x - y}{x + y}$. If $3 \otimes k = 3.5$ then $k =$

    (A) $-\frac{15}{7}$

    (B) $-\frac{5}{3}$

    (C) $-\frac{3}{2}$

    (D) -1

    (E) $-\frac{15}{13}$

21. If $20^{k-1} = 4^3 \cdot 5^3$, then $k =$

    (A) 4
    (B) 3
    (C) 2.5
    (D) 2
    (E) 1.8

GO ON TO THE NEXT PAGE

22. If $x + 7(2 - x) = 6(2 - x) + 3(x - 2)$, then $x =$

   (A) $\dfrac{8}{3}$

   (B) 0

   (C) -3

   (D) $-\dfrac{7}{3}$

   (E) -4

23. The circle in Figure 6 has center O and radius r. According to the figure, which of the following equations must a, b, and r satisfy?

   (A) $a + b = 2r$
   (B) $a^2 + b^2 = r^2$
   (C) $a^2 + b^2 = 2r^2$
   (D) $a^2 + b^2 = 4r^2$
   (E) $a^2 + b^2 = 8r^2$

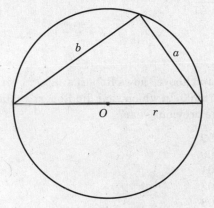

Figure 6

24. If a third of a circle's area is 6, then the circle's radius must be equal to

   (A) 2.39
   (B) 3.02
   (C) 3.14
   (D) 3.26
   (E) 4.07

25. If $f(x) = x^2 + 1$, $g(x) = 3x - 2$, and $h(x) = \dfrac{1}{2}x$, then $f(g(h(8))) =$

   (A) 55.5
   (B) 67
   (C) 93.2
   (D) 100
   (E) 101

GO ON TO THE NEXT PAGE

USE THIS SPACE FOR SCRATCHWORK.

26. A line segment connects the origin to the point (a, a^2). What is the slope of a line perpendicular to this line segment?

    (A) $-a$

    (B) $-\dfrac{1}{a}$

    (C) $2a$

    (D) $\dfrac{a^2 - 1}{a}$

    (E) $\dfrac{a}{a^2 + 1}$

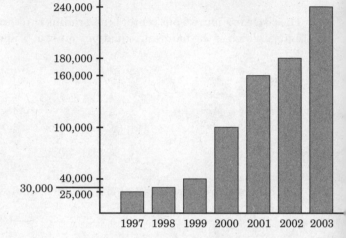

27. The graph above shows Robert's salary over the period from 1997 to 2003. In which year did Robert's salary increase by 60% over the previous year?

    (A) 1999
    (B) 2000
    (C) 2001
    (D) 2002
    (E) 2003

28. In Figure 7, if the length of AC is 15 and if $\angle CAB = 69°$, then what is the length of BC?

    (A) 33.2
    (B) 39.1
    (C) 41.7
    (D) 44.0
    (E) 44.8

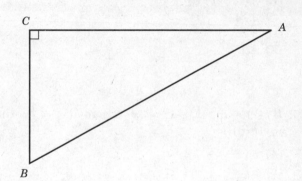

Figure 7

29. The geometric mean of two positive integers, a and b, is defined by $G_{ab} = \sqrt{a \cdot b}$. How many ordered pairs of positive integers (a, b) satisfy $G_{ab} = 3$?

    (A) One
    (B) Two
    (C) Three
    (D) Four
    (E) Infinitely many

GO ON TO THE NEXT PAGE

USE THIS SPACE FOR SCRATCHWORK.

30. x and y are real numbers, and $i^2 = -1$. If
$(x + iy) \cdot i + 3 = 2i + 6$, then $y =$

(A) -3
(B) 8
(C) 9
(D) $2i$
(E) $-6i$

31. The formula for the total surface area of a right circular cone
with equal radius and height is given by $SA(r) = \pi r(r + \sqrt{2r^2})$,
where r is the radius of the cone. If a cone has a radius and
height equal to 7, which of the following is the best
approximation of the surface area?

(A) 249
(B) 254
(C) 298
(D) 370
(E) 372

32. The average grade on a history test was 80. If 2 students had
each scored 10 points higher than they actually did, then the
average would have been 82. How many students are in the
class?

(A) 7
(B) 8
(C) 9
(D) 10
(E) 12

33. If $f(x) = \dfrac{1}{\sqrt{5 - 4x}}$, which of the following is in the domain of f?

(A) $-\dfrac{5}{4}$

(B) $\dfrac{5}{4}$

(C) $\dfrac{3}{2}$

(D) 2

(E) $\dfrac{7}{3}$

GO ON TO THE NEXT PAGE

34. Set A has 20 elements, and Set B has 60 elements. If Sets A and B have 7 elements in common, then what fraction of the total number of elements are in Set A only?

(A) $\dfrac{13}{80}$

(B) $\dfrac{13}{73}$

(C) $\dfrac{13}{40}$

(D) $\dfrac{7}{13}$

(E) $\dfrac{7}{12}$

35. For which of the following quadratic equations is the sum of the roots equal to -7 and the product of the roots equal to -33?

(A) $x^2 - 33x + 7 = 0$
(B) $x^2 - 7x + 33 = 0$
(C) $x^2 - 7x - 33 = 0$
(D) $x^2 + 7x + 33 = 0$
(E) $x^2 + 7x - 33 = 0$

36. Which of the following is the graph of the solution set to $2 \le |x| \le 3$?

(A)

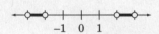

(B)

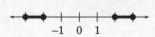

(C)

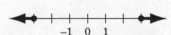

(D)

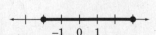

(E)

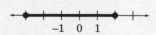

GO ON TO THE NEXT PAGE

37. In Figure 8, $\triangle ABC$ is similar to $\triangle DEF$ and DE is parallel to AC. If $\triangle ABC$ is an equilateral triangle with sides of length 3 then what is the perimeter of $\triangle DEF$?

(A) 3.14
(B) 3.33
(C) 3.5
(D) 4
(E) 4.5

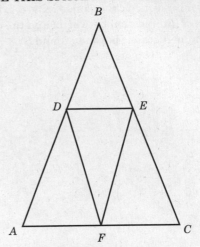

Note: Figure not drawn to scale.

Figure 8

38. $-3\cos^2\theta + (4 - 3\sin^2\theta) =$

(A) -1
(B) 0
(C) 1
(D) $2\sin^2\theta$
(E) $4 + \cos^2\theta$

39. What is the angle between the lines $3x - 4y = 7$ and $8x + 6y = 2$?

(A) $30°$
(B) $45°$
(C) $60°$
(D) $90°$
(E) Not enough information to tell

40. If $\log_{16}8 = x$, then $x =$

(A) $\dfrac{3}{4}$

(B) $\dfrac{4}{3}$

(C) $\dfrac{3}{2}$

(D) 2

(E) $\dfrac{5}{2}$

GO ON TO THE NEXT PAGE

41. Line l intersects a cube of side length 3. If A and B are two points of intersection between l and the cube, then what is the maximum distance between A and B?

    (A) $\frac{3}{2}$

    (B) 3

    (C) $3\sqrt{2}$

    (D) $3\sqrt{3}$

    (E) $3\sqrt{5}$

42. If the point $(6, -3)$ is on the graph of $y = f(x)$, and if $f(x)$ is defined for all real numbers, then which of the following points must be on the graph of $y = f(-x) - 1$?

    (A) $(-6, -4)$
    (B) $(-6, -3)$
    (C) $(-6, -2)$
    (D) $(6, -4)$
    (E) $(6, 4)$

43. If $0 < \theta < 90°$, then $\cot\theta \sin\theta \sec\theta =$

    (A) $\dfrac{1}{\cos\theta}$

    (B) $\sin\theta$

    (C) $\cot\theta$

    (D) -1

    (E) 1

44. The value of a car depreciates at a rate of 9% per year. If a car is worth \$22,000 in 1995, how much will it be worth in 2003?

    (A) \$9,772.25
    (B) \$10,345.56
    (C) \$12,456.81
    (D) \$14,287.43
    (E) \$16,101.75

GO ON TO THE NEXT PAGE

USE THIS SPACE FOR SCRATCHWORK.

45. The volume V of a regular polyhedron varies directly with the cube of the length of its sides. If the volume V is 100 when the polyhedron's sides are of length 3, then what is the volume when the sides are of unit length?

(A) 2.7
(B) 2.9
(C) 3.3
(D) 3.7
(E) 4.0

46. If $f(x) = \sqrt[3]{x-1} - 1$, what is the y-intercept of the graph of $f^{-1}(x)$?

(A) 0
(B) 1
(C) 2
(D) 3
(E) 3.3

47. In Figure 9, a regular hexagon is inscribed in a rectangle with sides of length 1 and $\frac{\sqrt{3}}{2}$. What is the length of the sides of the hexagon?

(A) $\frac{1}{4}$

(B) $\frac{1}{3}$

(C) $\frac{1}{2}$

(D) $\frac{2}{3}$

(E) $\frac{3}{4}$

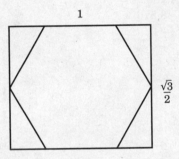

Figure 9

48. In Figure 10, if the area of parallelogram $ABCD$ is 49, which of the following could be the degree measure of θ ?

(A) 61°
(B) 66°
(C) 72°
(D) 79°
(E) 81°

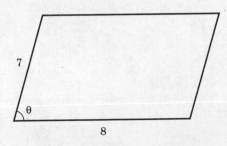

Note: Figure not drawn to scale.

Figure 10

GO ON TO THE NEXT PAGE

49. Figure 11 shows a cube with a volume of 64. If the cube is divided into two pieces along the plane through points A, B, C and D, then what is the total surface area of the resulting solids?

    (A) $96 + 32\sqrt{2}$
    (B) $96 + 32\sqrt{3}$
    (C) $96 + 64\sqrt{2}$
    (D) $96 + 96\sqrt{2}$
    (E) 192

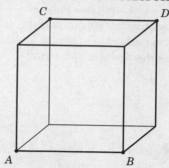

Figure 11

50. If the third term in a geometric sequence is 4 and the seventh term is 64, then what is the twentieth term in the sequence?

    (A) $65,536$
    (B) $131,072$
    (C) $262,144$
    (D) $524,288$
    (E) $1,048,576$

S T O P

IF YOU FINISH BEFORE TIME IS CALLED, YOU MAY CHECK YOUR WORK ON THIS TEST ONLY.
DO NOT TURN TO ANY OTHER TEST IN THIS BOOK.

SAT II Math IC
Practice Test 5
Explanations

Calculating Your Score

Question Number	Correct Answer	Right	Wrong	Question Number	Correct Answer	Right	Wrong	Question Number	Correct Answer	Right	Wrong
1.	E			18.	C			35.	E		
2.	D	——	——	19.	E			36.	B	——	——
3.	B	——	——	20.	B	——	——	37.	E	——	——
4.	A	——	——	21.	A	——	——	38.	C	——	——
5.	C	——	——	22.	A	——	——	39.	D	——	——
6.	D	——	——	23.	D	——	——	40.	A	——	——
7.	A	——	——	24.	A	——	——	41.	D	——	——
8.	C	——	——	25.	E	——	——	42.	A	——	——
9.	B	——	——	26.	B	——	——	43.	E	——	——
10.	E	——	——	27.	C	——	——	44.	B	——	——
11.	D	——	——	28.	B	——	——	45.	D	——	——
12.	A	——	——	29.	C	——	——	46.	C	——	——
13.	D	——	——	30.	A	——	——	47.	C	——	——
14.	B	——	——	31.	E	——	——	48.	A	——	——
15.	D	——	——	32.	D	——	——	49.	A	——	——
16.	A	——	——	33.	A	——	——	50.	D	——	——
17.	C	——	——	34.	B	——	——			——	——

Your raw score for the SAT II Math IC test is calculated from the number of questions you answer correctly and incorrectly. Once you have determined your composite score, use the conversion table on page 18 of this book to calculate your scaled score. To calculate your raw score, count the number of questions you answered correctly: _____
A

Count the number of questions you answered incorrectly, and multiply that number by $\frac{1}{4}$:

$$\underset{B}{\underline{\hspace{2cm}}} \times \frac{1}{4} = \underset{C}{\underline{\hspace{2cm}}}$$

Subtract the value in field C from value in field A: _____
D

Round the number in field D to the nearest whole number. This is your raw score: _____
E

Test 5 Explanations

Math IC Test 5 Explanations

1.   (E)   *Plane Geometry: Triangles; Algebra: Equation Solving*

The formula for the area of a triangle is $\frac{1}{2}bh$, where b is the triangle's base and h is its height. According to the question, the base and height of this triangle are equal, so you can write the area as $\frac{1}{2}b^2$. Set this expression equal to $18x^2$:

$$18x^2 = \frac{1}{2}b^2$$
$$36x^2 = b^2$$
$$6x = b$$

2.   (D)   *Fundamentals: Integers*

You need to know the basic properties of the integers for the Math IC. If a number is divisible by 2, 3, and 7, then it must also be divisible by the product of these numbers: $2 \times 3 \times 7 = 42$. Divide each of the answer choices by 42. Only choice (D) is not evenly divisible by 42, so it's the correct answer.

3.   (B)   *Algebra: Equation Solving*

The two lines intersect at the point when their x values are equal and their y values are equal. You can find the point of interesction by setting $y = x + 1$ and $y = 1 - x$ equal to each other:

$$1 - x = x + 1$$
$$0 = 2x$$
$$0 = x$$

4.   (A)   *Algebra: Equation Solving*

Solve for x by cross multiplying this equation:

$$\frac{2}{3x-1} = \frac{1}{13}$$
$$2(13) = 3x - 1$$
$$26 = 3x - 1$$
$$27 = 3x$$
$$9 = x$$

5.   (C)   *Algebra: Equation Solving*

The length of AD is equal to $AC + BD - BC$. Since AC and BD overlap on the segment BC, you need to subtract BC from the sum of AC and BD so you don't double count it.

$$AD = AC + BD - BC$$
$$= x + 2 + 12 - x - 3$$
$$= 14 - 3$$
$$= 11$$

6.　**(D)**　*Algebra: Equation Solving*

In order to find the value of x, you first need to find the value of y, since $x = y^2$. Start by plugging $z = 9$ into $y = \frac{z}{3}$:

$$y = \frac{9}{3}$$
$$= 3$$

Now plug this value of y into $x = y^2$:

$$x = 3^2$$
$$= 9$$

7.　**(A)**　*Coordinate Geometry: Lines and Slope*

The slope of a line is equal to its rise (change in y-value) over its run (change in x-value): $\frac{\Delta y}{\Delta x}$. In Figure 2, you can see that the endpoints of AB are $(2, 1)$ and $(4, 4)$. Use these points to determine the slope of the line segment. The segment's rise is $4 - 1 = 3$, and its run is $4 - 2 = 2$, so the slope $= \frac{\Delta y}{\Delta x} = \frac{3}{2}$.

8.　**(C)**　*Algebra: Polynomials*

When you have a polynomial in unfactored form, you should try factoring it since factoring often reveals a solution to the problem. In this case, factor the polynomial in the numerator:

$$\frac{x^2 + x - 6}{x + 3} = \frac{(x + 3)(x - 2)}{(x + 3)}$$
$$= x - 2$$

9.　**(B)**　*Algebra: Writing Equations, Word Problems*

The question tells you that you need x cups of flour for every 2 servings of food, and you can express this relationship as $\frac{x}{2}$ cups per serving. You need to figure out how many cups of flour you need in order to make 7 servings of food. Since the proportion of flour in the recipe should be the same whether you make 2 or 7 servings, you can set up the equation: $\frac{x}{2} = \frac{y}{7}$, where y is the number of cups of flour you need for 7 servings. Now solve for y:

$$\frac{7x}{2} = y$$

Finally, you need to convert this amount from cups per serving to quarts per serving:

$$\frac{7x}{2}\frac{\text{cups}}{\text{serving}} \times \frac{1 \text{ quart}}{4 \text{ cups}} = \frac{7x}{8}\frac{\text{quarts}}{\text{serving}}$$

10. **(E)** *Coordinate Geometry: Lines and Distance*

You should memorize the formula for finding the distance between points (x_1, y_1) and (x_2, y_2): $d = \sqrt{(x_1 - x_2)^2 + (y_1 - y_2)^2}$. Plug the points $(-3, -7)$ and $(4, 16)$ into this formula:

$$= \sqrt{(-3-4)^2 + (-7-16)^2}$$
$$= \sqrt{(-7)^2 + (-23)^2}$$
$$= \sqrt{49 + 529}$$
$$= \sqrt{578}$$
$$= 24.04$$

11. **(D)** *Plane Geometry: Triangles*

The triangle in the figure can be broken down into two right triangles:

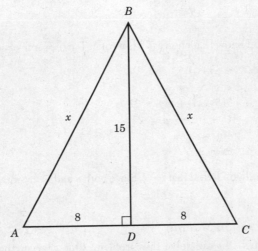

In order to find the perimeter of the large triangle, you first need to figure out the hypotenuse of one of the small right triangles. The small right triangles have legs of lengths 8 and 15. Use the Pythagorean Theorem to solve for the hypotenuse x:

$$x^2 = 15^2 + 8^2$$
$$= 255 + 64$$
$$= 289$$
$$x = 17$$

Now add up the sides of the large triangle to find the perimeter: $17 + 17 + 16 = 50$.

12. **(A)** *Plane Geometry: Lines and Angles; Trigonometry: Basic Functions*

Angles x and $2x$ are supplementary angles, which means that they add up to $180°$. You can solve for x using the equation $x + 2x = 180$.

$$3x = 180$$
$$x = 60$$

Now take the cosine of x, since $\angle DAB = x$: $\cos 60° = \frac{1}{2}$.

13. (D) *Algebra: Equation Solving*

This problem isn't particularly difficult, but it is time consuming. You can cut down on the time you spend by doing some quick elimination. For instance, you know that in choice (A) both n and m equal 1, since $n + m = 2$ and n and m are non-zero positive integers. But $3(1) + 7(1)$ does not equal 27, so you can eliminate choice (A). Similarly, for choice (B), which says that $n + m = 3$, you know that one of the variables must equal 1 and the other must equal 2. Now matter which of these values you assign to n and m, you can't produce $3n + 7m = 27$, so you can eliminate choice (B).

Now your fiddling with n and m becomes a little complicated. Take choice (C), which says that $n + m = 4$, and solve for n:

$$n = 4 - m$$

Plug this value for n into $3n + 7m = 27$:

$$3(4 - m) + 7m = 27$$
$$12 - 3m + 7m = 27$$
$$4m = 15$$
$$m = \frac{15}{4}$$

Since m is not an integer, you know that choice (C) is wrong. Try the same procedure on choice (D):

$$n + m = 5$$
$$n = 5 - m$$
$$3(5 - m) + 7m = 27$$
$$15 - 3m + 7m = 27$$
$$4m = 12$$
$$m = 3$$

Plug $m = 3$ into $n + m = 5$, and you'll find that $n = 2$. Since both n and m are integers, you know that choice (D) is correct.

14. (B) *Algebra: Equation Solving*

There are a number of ways you can solve this problem. One easy method is to create a common denominator, $3t$, on the left side of the equation:

$$\frac{1}{t} + \frac{2}{3t} = \frac{1}{3}$$

$$\frac{3}{3t} + \frac{2}{3t} = \frac{1}{3}$$

$$\frac{5}{3t} = \frac{1}{3}$$

Now cross multiply to get rid of the denominators:

$$15 = 3t$$
$$5 = t$$

15. **(D)** *Plane Geometry: Lines and Angles, Triangles*

To solve this problem, you need to know about the angles created by intersecting lines and the angles in a triangle. When you have two intersecting lines, the angles opposite each other are congruent, or equal:

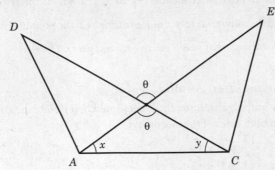

In the figure, $\angle DBE$ is equal to $\angle ABC$ because they are created by intersecting lines. $\angle ABC$ is the third angle in a triangle with angles x and y. Since the three angles in a triangle add up to $180°$, you can write the equation $x + y + \theta = 180$, or $\theta = 180 - x - y$.

16. **(A)** *Algebra: Writing Equations, Word Problems*

If John can paint a house in d days, then his rate of work is $\frac{1}{d}$ houses per day. Since work equals rate multiplied by time, in x days John paints $\frac{1}{d} \cdot x = \frac{x}{d}$. The amount of the house left unpainted is $1 - \frac{x}{d}$, since 1, or $\frac{d}{d}$, represents the completion of the house. Now turn $1 - \frac{x}{d}$ into a single fraction:

$$1 - \frac{x}{d} = \frac{d}{d} - \frac{x}{d}$$

$$= \frac{d - x}{d}$$

17. **(C)** *Coordinate Geometry: Lines and Slope*

The slope of a line is equal to the change in y-value divided by the change in x-value, or $\frac{y_1 - y_2}{x_1 - x_2}$. Plug the x and y values of $(k, k + 1)$ and $(2k, 2 - k)$ into the slope formula:

$$\frac{\Delta y}{\Delta x} = \frac{(2 - k) - (k + 1)}{2k - k}$$

$$= \frac{1 - 2k}{k}$$

Set this expression equal to $\frac{1}{3}$, and solve for k:

$$\frac{1}{3} = \frac{1 - 2k}{k}$$

$$k = 3 - 6k$$

$$7k = 3$$

$$k = \frac{3}{7}$$

18. **(C)** *Fundamentals: Integers; Statistics: Probability*

This problem is easier than it seems because you don't need to do any division. If a positive integer is divided by 5, then the set of all possible remainders is $\{0, 1, 2, 3, 4\}$. (If the remainder is greater than or equal to 5, then 5 can go into the number at least one more time.) Of the possible remainders, only $\{0, 2, 4\}$ are even integers. So the probability that you'll get an even integer is: $P(\text{even}) = \dfrac{3}{5}$.

19. **(E)** *Algebra: Inequalities, Absolute Value*

When solving an inequality with an absolute value, you should first isolate the absolute value on one side. In this case, subtract 3 from both sides of the inequality:

$$|x - 1| + 3 \le 0$$
$$|x - 1| \le -3$$

Here's the tricky part of the problem. By definition, the absolute value of any number or expression is a positive number, but this inequality states that the absolute value of $(x - 1)$ is negative. Since the absolute value cannot be a negative number, this inequality has no solution set.

20. **(B)** *Functions: Evaluating Functions*

This problem may seem intimidating because the function $x \otimes y$ is unfamiliar, but finding the solution is merely a matter of plugging values into the definition you're given. The question tells you that $x \otimes y = \dfrac{x - y}{x + y}$ and asks you to find $3 \otimes k$. Simply plug $x = 3$ and $y = k$ into $\dfrac{x - y}{x + y}$:

$$3 \otimes k = \frac{3 - k}{3 + k}$$

Now set this expression equal to 3.5 to find k:

$$\frac{3 - k}{3 + k} = 3.5$$
$$3 - k = 3.5(3 + k)$$
$$3 - k = 10.5 + 3.5k$$
$$-7.5 = 4.5k$$
$$k = -\frac{7.5}{4.5}$$
$$= -\frac{5}{3}$$

21. **(A)** *Algebra: Equation Solving, Exponents*

The fastest way to answer this question is to use the law of exponents that says $A^x \cdot B^x = (AB)^x$:

$$20^{k-1} = 4^3 \cdot 5^3$$
$$= (20)^3$$
$$20^{k-1} = 20^3$$

Since the bases of these two terms are equal, you know that their exponents must be equal:

$$k - 1 = 3$$
$$k = 4$$

22. (A) *Algebra: Equation Solving*

Distribute the terms in this equation to solve for x:

$$x + 7(2-x) = 6(2-x) + 3(x-2)$$
$$x + 14 - 7x = 12 - 6x + 3x - 6$$
$$14 - 6x = 6 - 3x$$
$$8 = 3x$$
$$\frac{8}{3} = x$$

23. (D) *Plane Geometry: Circles, Triangles*

If a triangle is inscribed within a circle such that one of the triangle's sides passes through the circle's origin, then the triangle must be a right triangle. In these cases, the triangle's hypotenuse is the circle's diameter. Since the diameter of the circle is twice the length of the radius r, you know that the hypotenuse is equal to $2r$. The question asks you to find an equation that must always be true of the triangle's sides, a, b, and r. Since the Pythagorean Theorem applies to all right triangles, you know the triangle's sides must conform to the following equation:

$$a^2 + b^2 = (2r)^2$$
$$a^2 + b^2 = 4r^2$$

24. (A) *Plane Geometry: Circles*

The area of a circle with radius r is given by the formula $A = \pi r^2$. Since a third of the circle's area is equal to 6, you can set up the following equation:

$$\frac{1}{3}A = 6$$
$$\frac{1}{3}\pi r^2 = 6$$
$$r^2 = \frac{18}{\pi}$$
$$r = \sqrt{\frac{18}{\pi}}$$
$$= 2.39$$

25. (E) *Functions: Compound Functions*

When solving compound functions like $f(g(h(8)))$, you need to work from the inside out. First evaluate $h(8)$ by plugging $x = 8$ into $h(x)$:

$$h(x) = \frac{1}{2}x$$
$$h(8) = \frac{8}{2}$$
$$= 4$$

Now plug 4 into $g(x)$:

$$g(x) = 3x - 2$$
$$g(4) = 3(4) - 2$$
$$= 10$$

Finally, plug 10 into $f(x)$:

$$f(x) = x^2 + 1$$
$$f(10) = 10^2 + 1$$
$$= 101$$

26. (B) *Coordinate Geometry: Lines*

The slopes of perpendicular lines are negative reciprocals of each other. If one line has a slope of m, then the other line has a slope of $-\dfrac{1}{m}$. To solve this problem, first find the slope of the line segment that connects the origin, $(0, 0)$, to the point (a, a^2). The slope of a line is defined as the change in y over the change in x. In this case, the slope is $\dfrac{\Delta y}{\Delta x} = \dfrac{a^2 - 0}{a - 0} = \dfrac{a^2}{a} = a$. The negative reciprocal of a is the slope of the perpendicular line: $m_\perp = -\dfrac{1}{a}$.

27. (C) *Fundamentals: Percents*

You need to find the year when Robert's salary increased by 60% — in other words, the year when it was 1.6 times larger than his salary the year before. According to the chart, his salary in 2001 was \$160,000 and his salary in 2000 was \$100,000. $1.6 \times 100,000 = 160,000$, so choice (C), 2001, is correct.

28. (B) *Trigonometry: Basic Functions*

Redraw the figure, including the information stated in the question:

This question tests your understanding of the basic functions of trig. In the right triangle above, you know the size of an angle and the length of the side adjacent to the angle. You're asked to find x, the length of the side opposite the given angle. The trig function that combines these elements is $\tan\theta = \dfrac{\text{opposite}}{\text{adjacent}}$. Plug the values you have into this function:

$$\tan 69° = \frac{x}{15}$$

$$15\tan 69° = x$$

$$x = 39.1$$

29. **(C)** *Algebra: Equation Solving; Fundamentals: Integers*

This question doesn't really involve the geometric mean. All you need to do is set the equations $G_{ab} = \sqrt{a \cdot b}$ and $G_{ab} = 3$ equal to each other:

$$3 = \sqrt{a \cdot b}$$

Now square both sides of the equation to get:

$$9 = a \cdot b$$

a and b are positive integers, and they must also be factors of 9. Since the positive integer factors of 9 are 1, 3, and 9, the possible pairs of a and b are $(1, 9)$, $(3, 3)$, and $(9, 1)$.

30. **(A)** *Miscellaneous Math: Complex Numbers*

Complex numbers come in the form $a + bi$, where a and b are real numbers and $i = \sqrt{-1}$. They consist of a real part, a, and an imaginary part, bi. When you have an equation involving two complex numbers, you can split the equation apart, equating the real parts with each other and the imaginary parts with each other. You can use this method to solve for x and y in this problem, but first you need to simplify the left side of the equation into the form $a + bi$:

$$(x + iy)i + 3 = 2i + 6$$
$$xi + i^2 y + 3 = 2i + 6$$

Since $i^2 = -1$, you can rewrite the left side as:

$$xi - y + 3 = 2i + 6$$

Now solve for y by equating the real components (the parts without i) of the equation:

$$-y + 3 = 6$$
$$y = -3$$

31. **(E)** *Functions: Evaluating Functions*

Solving this problem doesn't involve any solid geometry. All you need to do to get the answer is evaluate the surface area function at $r = 7$. Plug $r = 7$ into $SA(r)$, and then round your answer to the nearest integer:

$$
\begin{aligned}
SA(7) &= \pi \cdot 7(7 + \sqrt{2 \cdot 7^2}) \\
&= \pi \cdot 7(7 + 7\sqrt{2}) \\
&= 372
\end{aligned}
$$

32.   **(D)**   *Algebra: Writing Equations, Arithmetic Mean*

The average test score is equal to the sum of all the scores divided by the number of students who took the test. If T is the sum of all the scores and s is the number of students who took the test, then the average test score is $\frac{T}{s} = 80$, or $T = 80s$. Since you know neither T nor s, you need to write another equation to determine how many students are in the class. If two of the students had scored 10 points higher than they did, the average test score would have been 82 and the sum of all scores would have been 20 points higher than it was, or $80s + 20$. You can set up an equation for this new average:

$$\frac{80s + 20}{s} = 82$$

$$80s + 20 = 82s$$

$$2s = 20$$

$$s = 10$$

There are 10 students in the class.

33.   **(A)**   *Functions: Domain and Range*

The domain of a function $f(x)$ is all the values of x that produce real values of $f(x)$. Try plugging each of the answer choices into the function, and remember that the function is undefined when the denominator is zero or when the number under the square root sign is negative. When you plug in choice (A), you'll see that the function is defined for $x = -\frac{5}{4}$, so (A) is the correct answer.

$$f\left(-\frac{5}{4}\right) = \frac{1}{\sqrt{5 - 4\left(-\frac{5}{4}\right)}}$$

$$= \frac{1}{\sqrt{5 + 5}}$$

$$= \frac{1}{\sqrt{10}}$$

34.   **(B)**   *Miscellaneous Math: Sets*

Set A has 20 elements, and Set B has 60, but they overlap in 7 of these elements. The total number of elements in Set A and Set B is equal to the sum of A and B minus the 7 overlapping elements: $20 + 60 - 7 = 73$ elements total. You need to subtract 7 from the sum so you don't double count any elements. Since the question asks what fraction of the total elements are in Set A only, you need to determine the number of elements exclusively in Set A. Subtract the 7 overlapping elements from the 20 elements in Set A: $20 - 7 = 13$. So the fraction of elements in Set A only is $\frac{13}{73}$.

35. **(E)** *Algebra: Polynomials*

For a quadratic equation $ax^2 + bx + c = 0$, the sum of the roots is equal to $-\frac{b}{a}$ and the product of the roots is equal to $\frac{c}{a}$. Since you're looking for a quadratic where the sum of the roots is –7 and the product of the roots is –33, you can set up the equations $-\frac{b}{a} = -7$ and $\frac{c}{a} = -33$. Since $a = 1$ in all of the answer choices, you can simplify these equations to $b = 7$ and $c = -33$. If you plug these coeffients into $ax^2 + bx + c = 0$, you'll get choice (E): $x^2 + 7x - 33 = 0$.

36. **(B)** *Algebra: Inequalities*

An inequality that involves an absolute value has two solutions. One solution of $2 \le |x| \le 3$ is $2 \le x \le 3$. To find the second solution, multiply $2 \le x \le 3$ by –1, and remember that multiplying inequalities by negative numbers flips the inequality signs. The second solution is $-2 \ge x \ge -3$. On a number line graph, $2 \le x \le 3$ and $-2 \ge x \ge -3$ look like this:

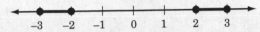

37. **(E)** *Plane Geometry: Triangles*

Figure 8 is misleading because it's not drawn to scale. Redraw $\triangle ABC$ as an equilateral triangle, and since $\triangle ABC$ is similar to $\triangle DEF$, make $\triangle DEF$ equilateral as well.

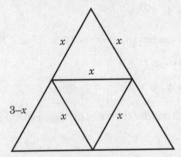

If $\triangle DEF$ is equilateral, then each side of the triangle has length x. $\triangle ADF$ must also be equilateral since DE and AC are parallel. Since the triangle's sides are equal, you can write $3 - x = x$ and get $x = \frac{3}{2}$. The perimeter of $\triangle DEF = 3\left(\frac{3}{2}\right)$, which is $\frac{9}{2}$ or 4.5.

38. **(C)** *Trigonometry: Pythagorean Identities*

The Pythagorean Trigonometric Identities will help you simplify seemingly complicated trig problems on the Math IC. The identity that's tested most frequently is $\sin^2\theta + \cos^2\theta = 1$. To solve this problem, isolate $\sin^2\theta + \cos^2\theta$:

$$
\begin{aligned}
-3\cos^2\theta + (4 - 3\sin^2\theta) &= -3\cos^2\theta + 4 - 3\sin^2\theta \\
&= -3(\cos^2\theta + \sin^2\theta) + 4 \\
&= -3(1) + 4 \\
&= -3 + 4 \\
&= 1
\end{aligned}
$$

39. **(D)** *Coordinate Geometry: Lines and Slope*

Solving for the angle between lines can be very tricky, so you should suspect that there's an easier way to answer this problem. The best way to solve this problem is to rearrange the equations of the lines in slope-intercept form, $y = mx + b$, where m is the slope of the line. First, rearrange the equation $3x - 4y = 7$:

$$3x - 4y = 7$$

$$y = \frac{3}{4}x - \frac{7}{4}$$

Now rearrange the second equation:

$$8x + 6y = 2$$

$$y = -\frac{4}{3}x + \frac{1}{3}$$

As you can see from these equations, the slopes are negative reciprocals of each other. Since perpendicular lines have negative reciprocal slopes, you know that these lines are perpendicular to each other; thus the angle between them is 90°.

40. **(A)** *Algebra: Equation Solving, Logarithms*

All you need to know to solve this problem is the definition of a logarithm: $\log_b a = x$ is equivalent to $b^x = a$. Rearrange the logarithm according to this definition and solve for x:

$$\log_{16} 8 = x$$

$$16^x = 8$$

Since 16 and 8 share the base 2, you can rewrite them as $16 = 2^4$ and $8 = 2^3$:

$$(2^4)^x = 2^3$$

$$2^{4x} = 2^3$$

Set the exponents equal to one another since the bases of both terms are equal:

$$4x = 3$$

$$x = \frac{3}{4}$$

41. **(D)** *Coordinate Geometry: Lines and Distance*

First draw a cube of side length 3.

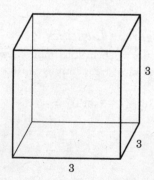

If A and B are two points on the cube, then the maximum distance between them is the long diagonal of the cube.

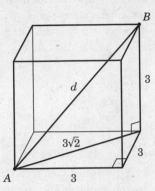

In order to calculate the long diagonal, you first need to find the diagonal of one of the cube's sides. Since the short diagonal creates a right triangle with the sides of the cube and since the cube's sides have length 3, you can use the Pythagorean Theorem to calculate the short diagonal, x:

$$x^2 = 3^2 + 3^2$$
$$x = 3\sqrt{2}$$

As you can see in the figure above, the short diagonal and the length of the cube form the legs of a right triangle with the long diagonal as its hypotenuse. Plug the short diagonal and the side length 3 into the Pythagorean Theorem to find the long diagonal, d:

$$d^2 = 3^2 + \left(3\sqrt{2}\right)^2$$
$$= 9 + 18$$
$$= 27$$
$$d = 3\sqrt{3}$$

42. **(A)** *Functions: Transformations and Symmetry*

You need to now how to transform graphs both vertically and horizontally. If you have the graph $y = f(x)$, then $y = f(-x)$ flips $y = f(x)$ across the y-axis. According to this rule, if (a, b) is on $y = f(x)$, then $(-a, b)$ must be on $y = f(-x)$. Also, if (a, b) is on $y = f(x)$, then $(a, b - 1)$ must be on $y = f(x) - 1$ since $f(x) - 1$ shifts the graph down by one unit. Now you can apply these rules to the function in the question. If $(6, -3)$ is on $y = f(x)$, then $(-6, -3)$ is on $y = f(-x)$. If $(-6, -3)$ is on $y = f(-x)$, then $(-6, -3 - 1)$, or $(-6, -4)$, is on $y = f(-x) - 1$.

43. **(E)** *Trigonometry: Basic Functions*

When you have a complicated trig expression, you should try to rewrite it in terms of sine and cosine. Use the trig definitions $\cot\theta = \dfrac{\cos\theta}{\sin\theta}$ and $\sec\theta = \dfrac{1}{\cos\theta}$ to simplify this problem:

$$\cot\theta\sin\theta\sec\theta = \frac{\cos\theta}{\sin\theta} \cdot \sin\theta \cdot \frac{1}{\cos\theta}$$

$$= \frac{\cos\theta}{\cos\theta} \cdot \frac{\sin\theta}{\sin\theta}$$

$$= 1$$

44. **(B)** *Algebra: Equation Solving, Exponential Growth and Decay*

You need to memorize the formula for exponential growth for the Math IC: $A(t) = A_o(1 + r)^t$, where A_o is the initial amount of an item, $A(t)$ is the amount after a period of time t, r is the rate of growth (in decimal form), and t is the period of time (usually in years). Plug the data given in the question into this formula. The initial value, A_o, of the car is $22,000. The value depreciates at 9% per year, so $r = 0.09$. The period of time, t, is 2003 – 1995 = 8 years.

$$A(8) = 22,000(1 - 0.09)^8$$
$$= 22,000(0.91)^8$$
$$= 10,345.56$$

45. **(D)** *Algebra: Writing Equations, Variation*

This question looks really hard because it involves some complicated solid geometry, but you actually don't need to use solid geometry to solve this problem. Instead, set up a direct variation equation. If the volume of the polyhedron varies directly with the cube of the length of its sides, then $V = k \cdot s^3$, where V is the polyhedron's volume, s is the length of the polyhedron's sides, and k is a constant. You can find k by plugging in $V = 100$ and $s = 3$:

$$100 = k \cdot 3^3$$
$$k = \frac{100}{27}$$

The question asks for the value of V when the polyhedron's sides are of unit length, or $s = 1$. Plug s and k into the variation equation to find V:

$$P = \frac{100}{27} \cdot (1)^3$$
$$= \frac{100}{27}$$
$$= 3.7$$

46. **(C)** *Functions: Inverse Functions*

The best way to solve this problem is to find $f^{-1}(x)$ and then plug in $x = 0$ to find its y-intercept. Finding the inverse function of $f(x)$ involves three steps. First, replace $f(x)$ with y:

$$f(x) = \sqrt[3]{x - 1} - 1$$
$$y = \sqrt[3]{x - 1} - 1$$

Second, switch x and y:

$$x = \sqrt[3]{y - 1} - 1$$

Last, solve for y:

$$x = \sqrt[3]{y - 1} - 1$$
$$x + 1 = \sqrt[3]{y - 1}$$
$$(x + 1)^3 = y - 1$$
$$(x + 1)^3 + 1 = y$$

This equation for y is the inverse function of $f(x)$. Plug $x = 0$ into the inverse function to find its y-intercept:
$f^{-1}(0) = (0 + 1)^3 + 1 = 2$.

47. **(C)** *Plane Geometry: Polygons*

Redraw Figure 9, labeling the sides of the hexagon:

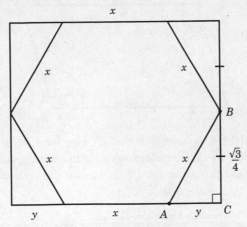

As you can see in the figure, the side of the hexagon is the hypotenuse of the right triangle ABC. In order to find the length of the side, you should figure out the length of the triangle's legs: BC and y. Since all of the hexagon's sides are equal, you know that B bisects the rectangle's side of length $\frac{3}{\sqrt{2}}$. Also, since B bisects the side, BC must be equal to half the side's length, or $BC = \frac{\sqrt{3}}{4}$. As you can also see from the figure, the rectangle's side of length 1 is equal to $y + x + y$, so you can set up the equation $2y + x = 1$, or $y = \frac{1-x}{2}$. Plug the legs of the right triangle into the Pythagorean Theorem to find the hypotenuse, x:

$$x^2 = \left(\frac{\sqrt{3}}{4}\right)^2 + \left(\frac{1-x}{2}\right)^2$$

$$x^2 = \frac{3}{16} + \frac{1}{4}(1 - 2x + x^2)$$

$$x^2 = \frac{3}{16} + \frac{1}{4} - \frac{1}{2}x + \frac{1}{4}x^2$$

$$\frac{3}{4}x^2 + \frac{1}{2}x - \frac{7}{16} = 0$$

Multipy through the equation by 16 to cancel out the denominator:

$$12x^2 + 8x - 7 = 0$$

$$(2x - 1)(6x + 7) = 0$$

$$x = \frac{-7}{6} \text{ or } x = \frac{1}{2}$$

Since it wouldn't make sense for the hexagon's sides to have a negative value, you know that the hexagon's sides must equal $\frac{1}{2}$.

48. **(A)** *Plane Geometry: Polygons*

Draw a picture of the parallelogram:

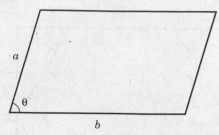

For the Math IC, you should definitely memorize the following formula for the area of a parallelogram: Area $= ab\sin\theta$, where a and b are the parallelogram's sides and θ is the included angle. You know that the parallelogram's area is 49 and its sides are 7 and 8, so you can plug these values into the area formula to find θ:

$$49 = 7 \cdot 8 \sin\theta$$

$$49 = 56\sin\theta$$

$$\frac{49}{56} = \sin\theta$$

Take the inverse sine of both sides of the equation:

$$\sin^{-1}\left(\frac{49}{56}\right) = \theta$$

$$61° = \theta$$

49. **(A)** *Solid Geometry: Prisms*

A cube's volume is equal to the cube of its sides, or s^3 when a cube has a side length of s. If the cube's volume is 64, then you can find the length of its sides using this volume formula:

$$s^3 = 64$$

$$s = 4$$

Draw a cube with sides of length 4 and include the plane that passes through points A, B, C, and D:

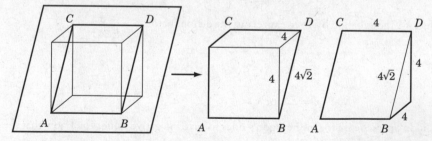

The plane divides the cube into two equal shapes. To calculate the total surface area of these solids, all you need to do is find the surface area of one solid and multiply it by two. Each solid has five sides. Two of the sides are squares of side 4. Calculate the surface area of these two squares: $2(4 \times 4) = 32$. Two of the sides are right triangles with base 4 and height 4. Calculate the surface area of these two triangles: $2\left(\frac{1}{2} \times 4 \times 4\right) = 16$. The fifth side is the polygon $ABCD$. You know that one of the polygon's sides, CD, is equal to 4, and you can find the other side using the Pythagorean Theorem:

$$(AC)^2 = 4^2 + 4^2$$
$$(AC)^2 = 32$$
$$AC = 4\sqrt{2}$$

To find the area of the polygon, multiply the sides together: $\text{Area}_{ABCD} = 4 \cdot 4\sqrt{2} = 16\sqrt{2}$. Find the total surface area by adding all these areas together and multiplying by 2: $2(32 + 16 + 16\sqrt{2}) = 96 + 32\sqrt{2}$.

50. **(D)** *Miscellaneous Math: Sequences*

Sequence problems rarely occur on the Math IC, but you should be prepared for when they do. The nth term in a geometric sequence is given by $a_n = a_1 \cdot r^{n-1}$, where a_n is the nth term, a_1 is the first term, and r is the constant ratio between terms. You're asked to find the 20th term in the sequence, but you know neither the value of the first term nor the ratio between terms. Since the question gives you the third term in the sequence ($a_3 = 4$), you can plug this value into the formula above to find a_1 in terms of the ratio r:

$$4 = a_1 \cdot r^{3-1}$$
$$4 = a_1 \cdot r^2$$
$$a_1 = \frac{4}{r^2}$$

The question also tells you the seventh term in the sequence: $a_7 = 64$. Plug a_7 into the formula to find another expression for a_1:

$$64 = a_1 \cdot r^{7-1}$$
$$64 = a_1 \cdot r^6$$
$$a_1 = \frac{64}{r^6}$$

Since both of these expressions equal a_1, you can set them equal to each other and find r:

$$\frac{4}{r^2} = \frac{64}{r^6}$$
$$\frac{r^6}{r^2} = \frac{64}{4}$$
$$r^4 = 16$$
$$r = 2$$

Now find a_1 by plugging r back into one of the equations:

$$a_1 = \frac{4}{r^2}$$

$$= \frac{4}{4}$$

$$= 1$$

Now that you have a_1 and r, you can find the 20th term in the sequence:

$$a_{20} = 1 \cdot 2^{20-1}$$

$$= 1 \cdot 2^{19}$$

$$= 524,288$$